TROPICAL FISH AQUARIUM

TROPICAL FISH AQUARIUM

FRESHWATER & MARINE

DAVID ALDERTON

This edition produced exclusively for
WHSMITH

Produced specially for W. H. Smith & Sons
by Ward Lock Limited, 82 Gower Street,
London WC1E 6EQ, a Pentos Company.

Text filmset in Baskerville
by A.K.M. Associates (U.K.) Ltd, Ajmal House,
Hayes Road, Southall, Greater London

Printed and bound in Spain by
Graficromo, S.A., Cordoba

Line illustrations drawn by Paul Saunders

CONTENTS

INTRODUCTION

Approximately 20,000 different species of fish, occurring in a wide range of habitats, are recognized by ichthyologists. The Blue Desert Fish (*Cyprinodon macularis*) is found in areas of water in the Nevada Desert of North America, where the temperature may reach 40°C (104°F). The Ice-fish (*Chaenocephalus*) of the Antarctic seas, in contrast, has developed chemicals in its blood which prevent it freezing to death.

Human interest in fish was first aroused by the realization that they could be used as a source of fresh food. Both the Egyptians and Romans harvested fish which they kept in artificial ponds. It was in the East, however, that ornamental fish-keeping developed as a hobby. Goldfish (*Carassius auratus*) were known in China by the tenth century, although they did not reach Britain until 700 years later. It is likely that ornamental strains of goldfish were derived from the wild form of carp (*C. carassius*), which was kept for food. Other colour forms of the goldfish were soon being developed and were given exotic names, such as 'Lotus Terrace' and 'Crane Pearl'. There was a particular pool near Peking that became known as 'Goldfish Pond'; it proved a popular spot, where visitors could see and admire many of these new varieties.

There was considerable interest in goldfish in other countries of the Orient, notably Japan, which ensured that European travellers to the East soon encountered these 'little gilded fish', as one seventeenth-century writer described them. Within 100 years, goldfish were breeding freely in Britain, and Horace Walpole was moved to write to his friend Montagu, requesting that he collected some goldfish soon, because Walpole himself was being overwhelmed with them.

Goldfish survive well in unheated surroundings, but by way of contrast, the Guppy (*Poecilia reticulata*), which is now the most widely-kept tropical fish, was not seen alive in Europe until 1908. This species occurs naturally in northern South America as well as on some offshore islands, and in less than a century, it too has been thoroughly domesticated and is currently being bred in many forms.

THE BOOM IN TROPICAL AQUARIA

The development of tropical fish-keeping as a popular hobby has occurred almost exclusively during the twentieth century. Prior to this, the difficulties encountered in maintaining tanks were almost insurmountable, and the supply of fish was minimal. The reasons underlying the boom in tropical aquaria are closely linked to the rapid developments in technology which have taken place in the present century.

Air transport has made it possible for fish to be flown large distances in a relatively short space of time, and to arrive at their destinations in good health. In 1976, for example, fish were imported from thirty-five countries into Britain. Singapore has become a major centre of the aquatic business, exporting no less than thirty-five million dollars worth of fish and three million dollars worth of aquatic plants during 1980 alone, giving it an estimated third of the world's total trade. Many aquarium fish are now bred commercially in fish farms, rather than being taken from the wild. In Florida, one such organization alone supplies approximately eighteen million fish to the trade annually. This is a long way removed from the early years of the century, when the few tropical fish which did reach Britain had to be sent from Europe by rail and sea, with over three-quarters of most consignments perishing *en route* during the two-day journey.

When tropical fish arrive at their destinations, electrical apparatus can be used to maintain their environment at a constant temperature and to help keep it clean and aerated. Since the 1960s, considerable strides have been made to facilitate the keeping of tropical fish in the home. Mass production of tanks and equipment, coupled with full utilization of new

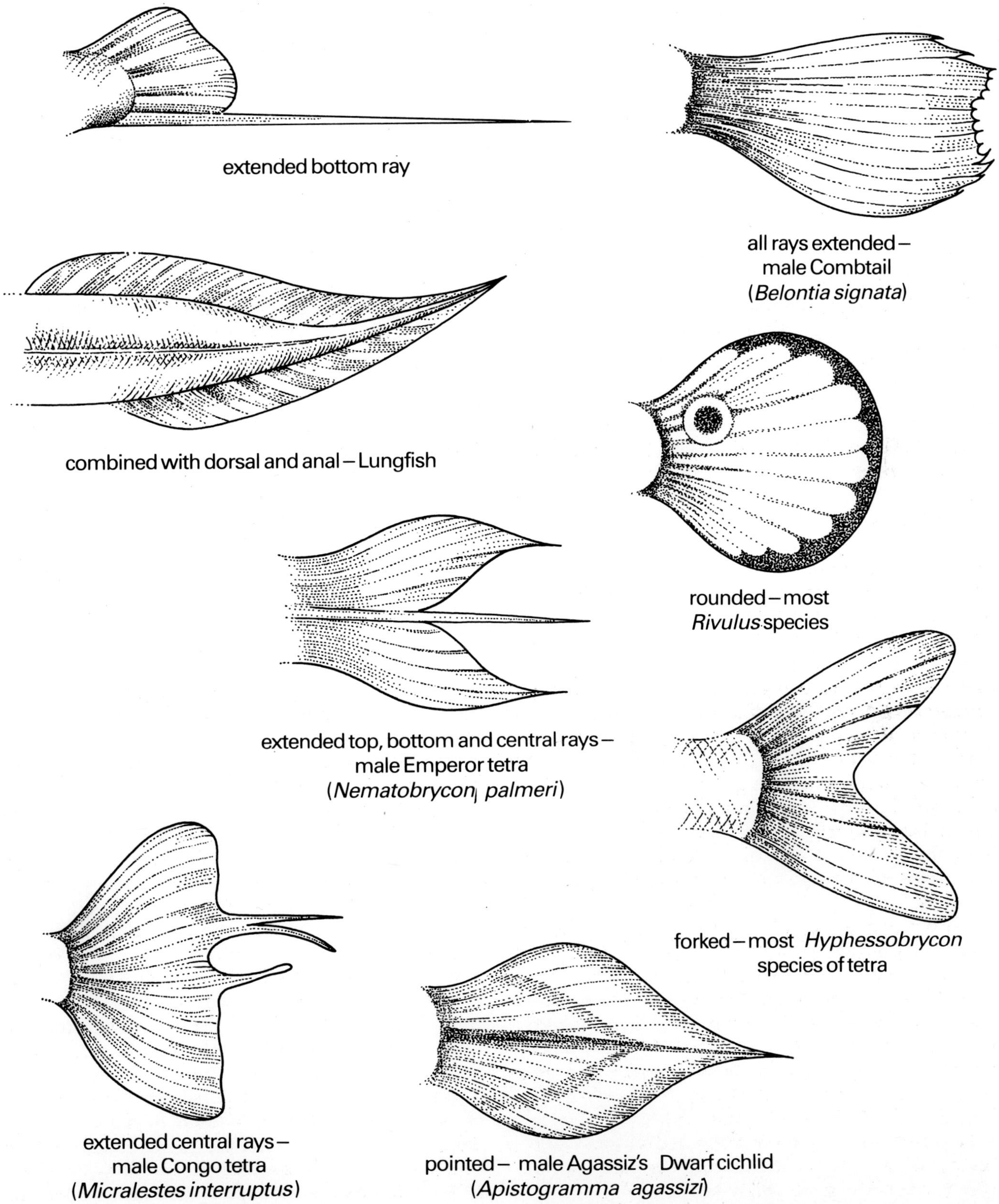
extended bottom ray
all rays extended – male Combtail (*Belontia signata*)
combined with dorsal and anal – Lungfish
rounded – most *Rivulus* species
extended top, bottom and central rays – male Emperor tetra (*Nematobrycon palmeri*)
forked – most *Hyphessobrycon* species of tetra
extended central rays – male Congo tetra (*Micralestes interruptus*)
pointed – male Agassiz's Dwarf cichlid (*Apistogramma agassizi*)

Fin types.

technology, have ensured that the cost of a tropical aquarium complete with fish is not prohibitive for the majority of people. In addition, costs involved in maintaining and feeding the fish are minimal.

An aquarium also lends itself to a twentieth-century lifestyle. Unlike most other creatures, fish can be kept without difficulty in a very wide variety of domestic environments, in flats or apartments, for example, where other pets would be impractical. Their tanks will fit attractively in various locations, whether recessed into a wall or used as a room-divider. In addition, fish-keeping is a relaxing hobby, and it is no coincidence that in potentially stressful places, such as a dentist's waiting-room, a tank of fish is often present.

There is considerable scope within the hobby for the enthusiast. Apart fom the wide array of both coldwater and tropical fish of all sizes and colours which are now available, there is the added interest of breeding them. Aquarist societies exist in many regions, and often organize shows for their members.

Angelfish (*Pterophyllum* sp.) occur in reedy areas.

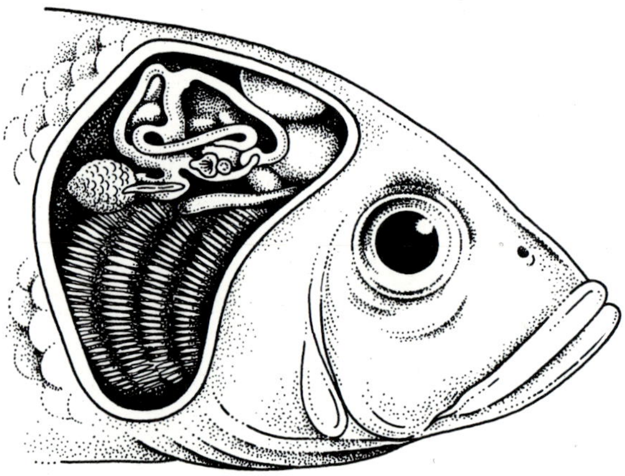

Head of Labyrinth fish cut away to illustrate the labyrinth organ, which enables these fish to breathe atmospheric air directly.

They also provide an ideal opportunity to meet people with a similar interest.

PISCINE CHARACTERISTICS

Fish occur in a wide range of aquatic environments, and observation of their shape will often give an indication of their habits. Those which live close to the bottom, such as loaches or eels, generally resemble worms. Tall, thin fish, like angelfish, are found in reedy localities, where they hide and weave in and out of the vegetation. Fish found near the surface have a relatively straight back and a rounded belly, as seen in the case of the hatchetfish of South America, whereas fish occurring in the main body of water are more streamlined. The position of the mouth is also indicative of a fish's living habits. In loaches, it points downwards, whereas it sticks up in hatchetfish. The number and type of teeth present depends on the fish concerned, but serve to reveal its feeding habits. The sharp teeth of the piranha are legendary, even to those who have never kept fish.

Fish rely largely on their gills to extract oxygen from the water. Other gases, such as carbon dioxide, are excreted by this route. The gills themselves are located behind the eyes, with the rows of filaments on each side protected by a cover. Modifications to this pattern of respiration are seen in certain fish. Anabantid or labyrinth fish are able to breathe atmospheric air directly through their gills, whereas others can utilize their swim-bladder, which is normally used for buoyancy, for respiratory purposes. Any interference with gill function is likely to have very serious effects on the fish itself.

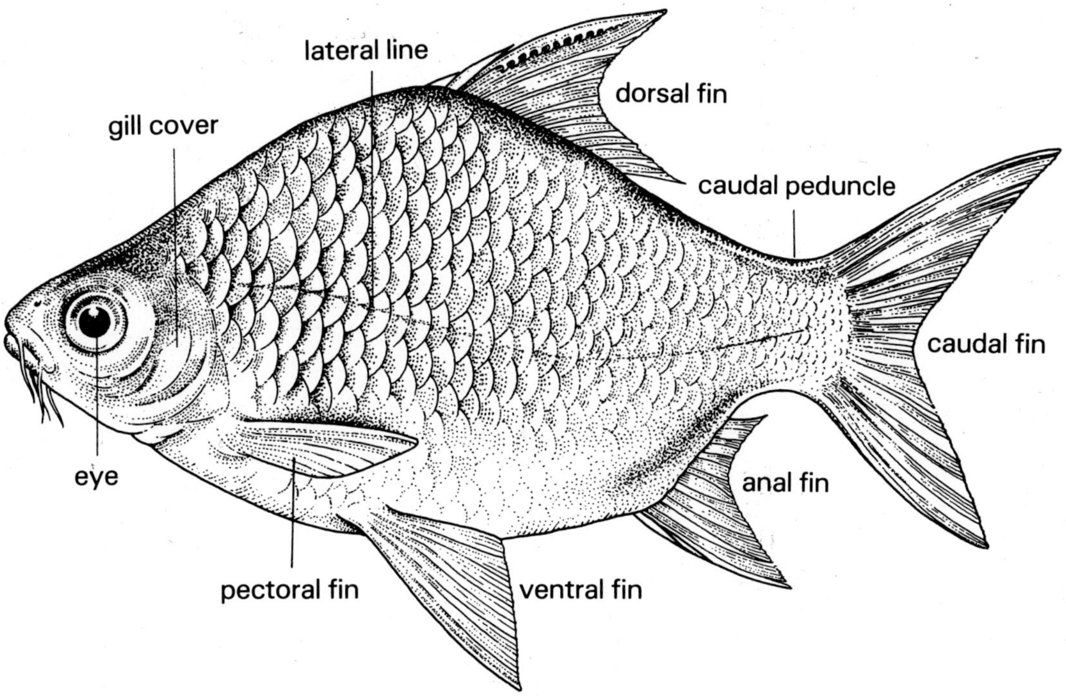

Anatomy of a fish.

Internal anatomy of a fish.

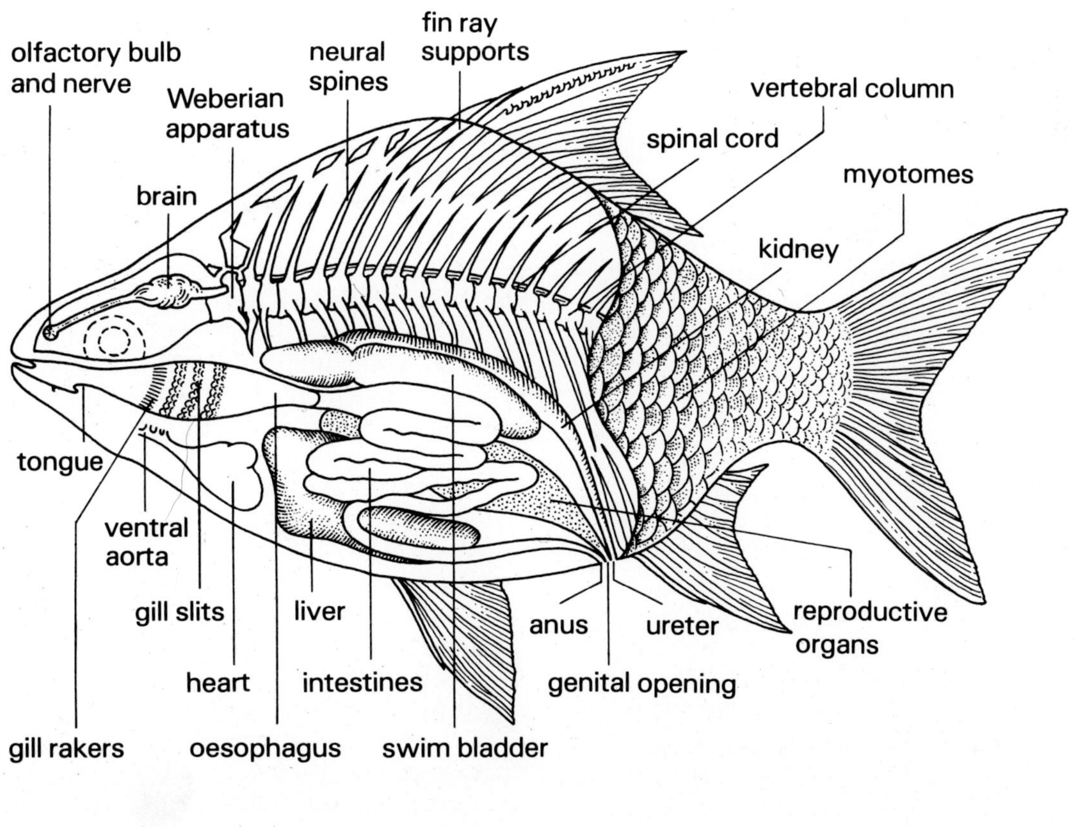

The fish's sensory system differs significantly from that of a mammal. The lateral line, which is visible along the length of the body in most fish, detects changes in pressure in the external environment. The presence of both stationary and moving objects can also be ascertained by this means. The pressure waves impinging on the fish's skin are transmitted via the mucus in the canal to neuromasts, and these cells are linked directly to the brain by cerebral nerves.

Sight is a variable sense in fish, ranging from virtual lack of vision in the case of Blind Cave Fish, to the highly developed visual acuity possessed by most fish that live near the water's surface. Whereas fish found in clear waters, around coral reefs for example, usually have good sight, fish occurring in murky surroundings, such as various catfish, have a keen sense of smell. They also have barbels in the vicinity of their mouth which contain taste buds. Fish can prove quite adaptable, as shown by a Spiny Catfish (*Acanthordoras spinosissimus*) born without eyes; it immediately managed to feed itself by smell alone, and lived satisfactorily for years.

Fish do not sleep in the same way as mammals, although in darkness they do become inactive, and body processes slow down. At dawn, they take approximately twenty minutes to become fully alert again, and often will not feed during this period. It is advisable to introduce new arrivals to an unlit aquarium as this will be less stressful; give them a short period to settle down before switching on the lighting.

Lifespan varies from one species of fish to another. Certain killifish may only survive a matter of months until their ponds dry up, but when kept in water constantly, some have lived for five years. Goldfish and catfish generally prove the longest-lived species under aquarium conditions, often living ten years or more. In the case of marine species, the French Angel and other members of the *Pomacanthus* genus can live for eight years or so. By way of contrast, seahorses naturally appear to have a short lifespan.

THE TRADE IN FISH

Although many aquarium freshwater fish are bred commercially, a proportion are still caught in the wild. The supply of such fish is often seasonal, because of trapping conditions. The collection of fish in the Amazon Basin, for example, takes place during the dry season, when the water level is low and the fish are concentrated in particular places. New species are still being discovered: over half the specimens captured by one expedition during the late 1970s from the Matto Grosso region of Brazil were previously unknown.

Aphyosemion sjoestedtii. These killifish from West Africa live only a short period, before the water in their pools evaporates.

Many fish are caught for the trade with nets, which are spread around the roots of floating plants. Discus, cichlids and angelfish are easily netted in this way. They are then transferred to barrels on the natives' boats, and taken to an exporter, who makes up the orders for despatch. The fish are packed with oxygen and a tranquillizer in their water, before being flown out to their eventual destinations. Movement of fish from one country to another may be regulated by both health and conservation controls, so advice should be sought from the relevant authorities in advance.

Commercial breeding of marine fish and invertebrates has yet to be achieved on a significant scale, so the vast majority of these creatures which are imported will be wild-caught. It is to be hoped that this situation will soon alter, lessening the pressure on wild stocks, and ensuring that healthier stock is available to aquarists.

Fish should move without any apparent difficulty, swimming evenly through the water. You should avoid any individuals with ragged or frayed fins if at all possible; drooping fins are also indicative of ill-thrift, although in certain cases, such as Fighting Fish, this condition is quite normal. The eyes must not protrude unnaturally from their sockets, as this state, known as 'pop-eye', is a sign of illness. The scales should appear healthy, and show no signs of white spots or fungus. Larger parasites, such as *Argulus*, may occasionally be seen on the sides of fish, especially goldfish, and these can present problems. Most dealers go to great trouble to ensure that their stock is healthy, but there are exceptions, and shops where dead fish are left floating in tanks alongside apparently healthy individuals should not be patronized. Although the remaining fish in the tank may appear healthy, the chances of their succumbing to disease, following the stress of being moved, are increased.

PART I

THE FRESHWATER AQUARIUM

1 TANKS AND EQUIPMENT

The traditional rectangular tank, constructed with an iron frame and using putty to hold the glass in place, is now a rare sight in aquarist shops. The advent of silicone rubber sealant has led to a revolution in the design of tanks over the last two decades, enabling a much wider range of shapes to be created, freed from the constraints of an iron framework. Triangular tanks for example, to fit neatly in the corner of a room, are now seen quite often.

AQUARIUM SEALANTS

Whereas putty tends to dry out, causing the tank to leak, silicone rubber, having been applied to the glass surfaces and left to cure in air for forty-eight hours, forms a permanent bond. It does not set hard but remains flexible, and is thus able to absorb different water pressures without its bonding power being compromised. With normal, slight temperature changes causing both contraction and expansion in the glass of the tank, this is vital. When epoxy resin was tried as a tank sealer, leaks developed because the bonding was too rigid.

FRAMELESS TANKS

As silicone rubber has a bonding power of 2068 kN per sq m (300 lb per sq in), the heavy iron framework of putty tanks is no longer required, and tanks are lighter and cheaper as a result. Most people prefer to purchase a ready-made tank, but it is quite easy to make one to specific dimensions. The size of the tank will be influenced in either case by the space available for it, and the fish which are to be kept in it. Adequate allowance must be made for the fishes' subsequent growth, so it is advisable to obtain a large tank from the outset.

TANK SIZES

The dimensions of the tank that give rise to the surface area of the water, the length and width, are important because this is where atmospheric oxygen diffuses into the water. If the length and width of the tank are too small, relative to its depth, then, when a large number of fish are present, the water may contain insufficient oxygen to support them. Although deep tanks are necessary for large, tall fish, like angelfish, it becomes progressively harder to light the lower levels effectively from above as the depth increases.

When recommendations are made for the volume of water to be allowed per unit length of fish, they should not be considered as absolute figures; they are given as guidelines. A tank that is stocked to its maximum limit at the outset will soon be overcrowded as its occupants increase in size.

It is easy to calculate the volume of a tank, especially if metric dimensions are used. Multiply the length by the width by the depth, in centimetres, then divide the total by 1000, to obtain the tank's capacity in litres. Subtract 10 per cent to allow for tank decoration, and you will have the functional capacity. For small fish, an allowance of 1½–2 litres per centimetre of length should be adequate, or approximately 1 gallon per inch using imperial units. A 30 litre tank will therefore support fish whose combined lengths do not exceed 15 cm (6 in). You will need to know the true capacity of the tank if you have to add any treatments to the water, to ensure that the correct dilution is obtained.

PLASTIC TANKS

Plastic tanks moulded as a complete unit are lighter than a glass design of similar dimensions. Unfortunately, the plastic sides scratch very easily and become unsightly, with debris and even algae sometimes accumulating in the depressions. The smaller rectangular designs are ideal for breeding tanks, and circular models are produced as goldfish tanks. These are free from the major, sometimes fatal, disadvantage of the old glass goldfish bowl, which had a narrow neck. If the latter were filled to the top, the surface area was much reduced, so the fish could suffer from an oxygen deficiency; whereas when only half full, although this gave a bigger surface area, the volume of water available for swimming was much reduced and planting was also less successful. Such bowls should never be used. Rectangular tanks are the best ones to choose whenever possible.

COVERING THE TANK

Hoods are manufactured to correspond with specific sizes of tank. They keep evaporative loss to a minimum, and help to reduce heating costs since the air above the water is maintained at a relatively constant temperature. A hood will also prevent more active fish, such as Oscars, from jumping out of the tank, and it reduces contamination of the water by household dust. If a hood of any kind is used with an angle-iron framed tank, small plastic clips should be used to prevent the two surfaces coming into direct contact, because condensation may drip onto the iron frame causing it to rust along its upper surface. This occurs especially when just a sheet of glass is used as a cover.

LIGHTING

The majority of hoods include space for an electric light, often with a raised surrounding area, known as a reflector, which should spread the light evenly over the water surface. The usual incandescent domestic light bulb can be fitted, but these do not last very long under such conditions as they are designed to hang vertically, rather than horizontally. They also give out unwanted heat on to the surface of the water, and are relatively expensive to operate compared to fluorescent lighting.

Fluorescent tubes, which are produced in a range of sizes, are the most popular choice for illuminating aquaria. Although they are expensive, '*Gro-Lux*' and similar tubes, which emit light from the red and blue parts of the spectrum thus closely imitating natural light, are of great value especially above a planted tank. They encourage healthy plant growth, and

Spotted Headstander (*Chilodus punctatus*). These fish will attempt to leap out of the tank if they are overcrowded.

Three types of tank hood; the top one has a fluorescent tube fitted in place. A plastic splash cover, to protect the light, can be fitted below the hood. It will also prevent active fish from leaping up and burning themselves on the light.

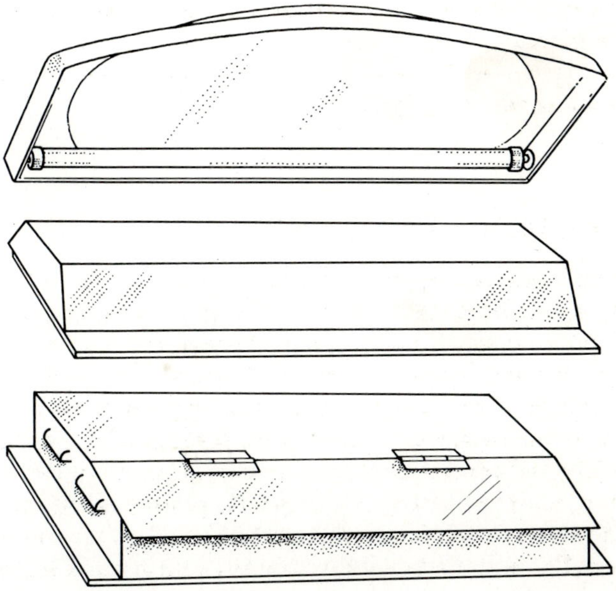

emphasize the colour of the fish to good advantage, with reds and blues becoming particularly prominent.

The optimum amount of light that will be required is largely a matter of trial and error (as explained later), and the length of time that artificial illumination is needed for must be adjusted, according to individual circumstances, to prevent excessive algal growth. The lighting can be controlled by a time switch, so that it will come on and off automatically.

D.I.Y. TANK CONSTRUCTION

Silicone rubber sealant is available in tubes, with an attached nozzle dispenser, for the prospective tank-builder; it can also be used for repairing tanks. It is important to use aquarium sealant only, as other types may contain chemicals which are toxic to fish. The saving in cost of building one's own tank against that of commerically-produced models is, however, usually marginal, unless an unusual design is required. The choice of glass for the tank is a vital consideration, both with regard to stability, and clarity of viewing. A minimum thickness of 6.4 mm (¼ in) should be used to form the tank's bottom, and 9.5 mm (⅜ in) is best for 120 cm (48 in) tanks. As an additional safeguard for all tanks over 60 cm (24 in) in length, a supporting beam should be positioned half-way along the top, running from front to back. Alternatively, extra support can be given lengthways by strips running from end to end on the two main panels. These strips can also help to support the tank cover if they are positioned just below the top of the tank.

You should choose float glass for the front panel, but you can economize by using rough-cast glass for the remainder, although visibility will not be as good through these panels. Second-hand glass is not recommended because it may contain minute imperfections, in the form of scratches, which weaken it.

Having decided on the dimensions, and with the pieces of glass cut to size, the first stage is to smooth off the rough edges using fine-grade emery paper. Wet the glass surfaces at frequent intervals during this process, and wash them thoroughly when you have finished. When wet, the glass is particularly slippery, and needs to be handled with extra care. When the panels have dried, clean them with a solvent such as pure turpentine, to ensure that there are no remaining residues which could compromise the subsequent bonding of the silicone rubber with the glass. Finally, wipe the surfaces over again thoroughly with clean paper tissues before beginning to assemble the tank.

The actual construction of the tank is best carried out on a large table or clean workbench covered with newspaper to prevent the glass getting scratched. Lay the base panel flat on top of the paper, and draw out a thin line of sealant along one long edge. Take the glass that will form the front, and place it carefully in position, propping it up vertically from behind. Fix the sides to the base and front with sealant in the same way, and then tape them, on the outside, to the front. The final step is to fix the back of the tank in place, again taping this to the sides for extra support while the sealant is curing. Check that the whole unit is as square as possible, making any adjustments that are needed.

After leaving the tank for a day, you can seal it around the inside, but take care not to introduce bubbles of air into the seal. Strengthening bars, if necessary, should be inserted at this stage. Leave the tank for two more days, then remove the tape around the corners and test it to make sure that it does not leak, giving it a thorough washing out at the same time. Although it is possible to cut away excess sealant with a sharp razor blade or modelling knife, you should avoid doing this if possible because the seal may be damaged in the process. As explained in the next chapter, such tanks when filled must always rest on a bed of polystyrene.

CONTROLLING THE TEMPERATURE OF THE WATER

The development of safe, accurate and reliable aquarium heaters controlled by thermostats is one of the major factors that has led to the huge growth in popularity of tropical fish-keeping. Previously the dedicated enthusiast had to maintain the temperature of water by means of oil lamps, which often filled the room with fumes, or gas jets directed under the slate base of the tank.

The heater and thermostat can be purchased as either combined or separate units. The former arrangement is more straightforward, with less wiring involved, and is ideal for smaller tanks. In larger set-ups, however, where more than one heater is required, a separate thermostat in overall control may be preferable. External thermostats can be adjusted without disturbing the rest of the tank. Most thermostats are set around 25°C (77°F) following manufacture, but can be simply adjusted by a partial turn of a screw. Alterations to the setting may be necessary when treating an outbreak of disease, or when attempting to breed a particular species.

The design of both heaters and thermostats is being

updated rapidly owing to the benefits of silicon chip technology, which has revolutionized the whole electronics industry. The heating unit consists of an electric heating element encased in a glass tube, and it is available in various wattages, normally between 75 and 150 watts. The conventional thermostat has bimetallic strips, which open and close depending on the water temperature, switching the heater on or off respectively. Unfortunately these contacts eventually lose their accuracy, and may fuse together. The most modern units have no switches, and are thus more reliable and accurate, and longer lasting. A knowledgeable dealer will be able to advise on the best designs currently available, and it is a false economy to purchase the cheapest model.

The very latest development in aquarium heaters is the under-tank model, which came on the British market in 1983. As its name suggests, this thin heater, in the form of a pad only 0.625 cm ($\frac{1}{4}$ in) thick, fits underneath the tank. Such heaters are unobtrusive and transfer heat evenly throughout the aquarium. Several can be linked together to fit the base of a large tank. Water temperature is again controlled by a thermostat, preferably of the external type.

HEATING THE AQUARIUM

The size of heater required for a particular tank is calculated on the basis of 100 watts per 100 l (22 gal) of water in the normal room, but in colder surroundings where there is no external heating, an additional 50 watts per 100 litres should be allowed. You should make sure that the heater is not too powerful for the tank, as this will cause the thermostat to do more work; whereas a lower-wattage heater will be on for a longer period to maintain the water temperature, but will cause less switching via the thermostat.

THERMOMETERS

The correct functioning of the heater and 'stat', which is a common abbreviation for 'thermostat' amongst aquarists, must always be monitored by means of a thermometer. Various types are available, ranging from the traditional, coloured-alcohol thermometer, mounted in a protective glass tube with a scale, which attaches by means of a rubber sticker to the inside of the tank. Circular models, with a pointer and scale sealed in a rubber casing, are affixed in a similar way. These, however, perhaps because they are more bulky and have a reduced area of attach-

Separate thermostat (left) and heater (right). Both are enclosed in glass tubes. The apparatus must always be covered by water when it is switched on.

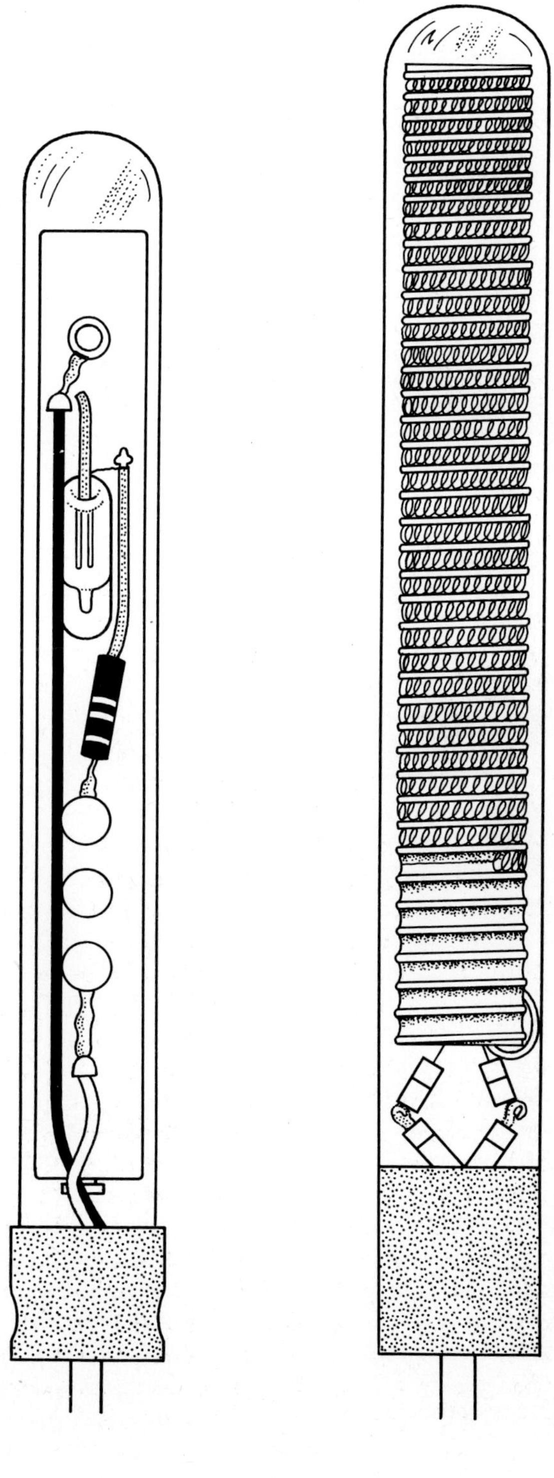

ment, do not seem to stick in place as well as the tubular type.

Digital thermometers, first introduced to aquarists around 1977, have become very popular in a relatively short space of time. They adhere via a sticky backing to a glass surface on the outside of the aquarium. The water temperature within is transmitted to the cholesteric compound present in the flat strip constituting the thermometer, and registers visually in large figures on a coloured background. These thermometers are extremely accurate, being calibrated to within half a degree, but once positioned they cannot be moved successfully. In addition, young curious fingers can alter the temperature display easily by touching the strip. The lifespan of a digital thermometer is somewhat shorter than that of the conventional spirit type, but the ease of reading is an advantage.

AIR PUMPS

Air pumps are used to circulate the water, rather than to introduce significant amounts of oxygen, and effective circulation will help to maintain a constant temperature throughout the tank. Air pumps for aquaria are marketed in a variety of sizes, and it is worth selecting a relatively expensive model, because cheaper designs are often more noisy when operating. Movement of water in the tank also ensures that debris and waste products from the fish can be removed via a filter. Pumps often have a dual role, forming part of a filtration system as well, so you should select a suitably powerful model.

The diaphragm pump is a popular type, used by many aquarists. It is operated by an electromagnet, which vibrates up and down when current enters it through a coil. In so doing, the magnet activates a diaphragm which draws air into the apparatus like a pair of bellows. The air then passes into the tank via tubing, with valves acting to even out the intermittent sucking effect of the diaphragm, thus establishing a constant air flow. Some models also include a rheostat, which indirectly controls the output of air by altering the input of power to the coil. As a result, the pump's action can be modified; it is quieter when less air is being drawn through it. The wattage of diaphragm pumps is extremely low, so the cost of running one round the clock, as will be necessary when it is connected to an undergravel filter, is negligible.

You should make sure that all the valves are kept clean. In addition, you should replace the diaphragm, which is a relatively simple task, at least annually.

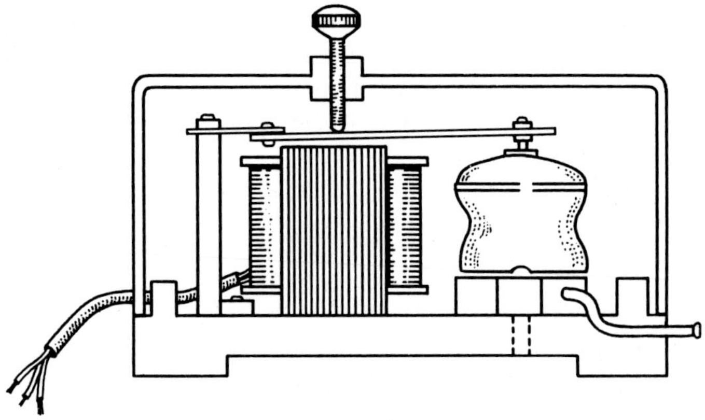

Diaphragm pump.

This should ensure quiet, trouble-free operation. Most pumps have a rubber base to reduce any noise resulting from vibration. If noise is a problem, place the unit on a pad of felt or similar material, which should help to quieten it. The pump must never be covered in any way while operating, because overheating will result with the subsequent likelihood of fire.

AIR-STONES AND AIR-LIFTS

The air pump can be connected up to air-stones, which break the air down into a constant stream of smaller bubbles. Alternatively, it can be connected to tank ornaments, such as clams or divers, which emit bubbles of gas at regular intervals. An air-lift provides

Air (diffuser) stone.

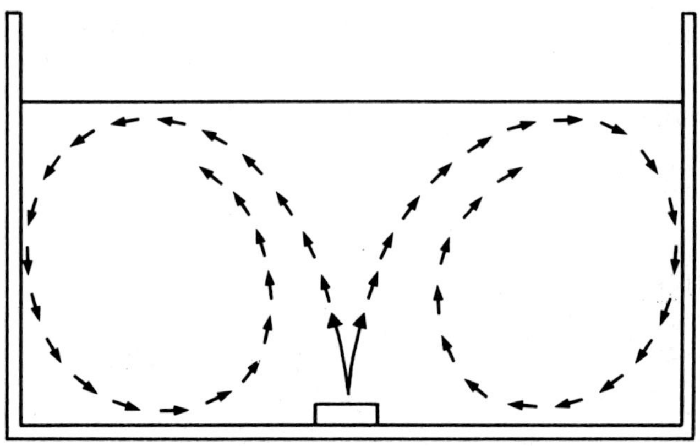

a refinement of this: it consists of a plastic tube set vertically in the tank to a height just below the surface. Air passes up this tube, forcing water up above the surface level at the same time. This water can then pass through a filter, or it can continue to circulate within the tank. Oxygenation at the surface is improved by this means.

METHODS OF FILTRATION

The purpose of filtration is to remove waste matter, which could otherwise build up and poison the tank's inhabitants. There are three systems of filtration available to aquarists, and it is not uncommon for two or more to be used simultaneously. Indeed, biological filtration occurs naturally in established tanks; bacteria present in the gravel degrade waste matter and potentially toxic compounds such as ammonia and nitrite, to nitrate, which can be taken up and utilized by the aquarium plants. For this system to work effectively, the bacteria must have adequate oxygen, and the tank must not be overcrowded; nor should the fish be overfed, as the surplus increases the level of contamination for the bacteria. Mechanical filtration is less complex. Solid material is removed and retained when the water passes through a medium such as filter wool, which needs to be changed regularly to remain effective. The third method is chemical filtration, which uses activated charcoal. This has a large surface area and absorbs dissolved organic waste products and other compounds into its many cracks and crevices. Filters used in aquaria rely on one or more of these means of filtration.

Substrate filtration with the water moving downwards through the substrate.

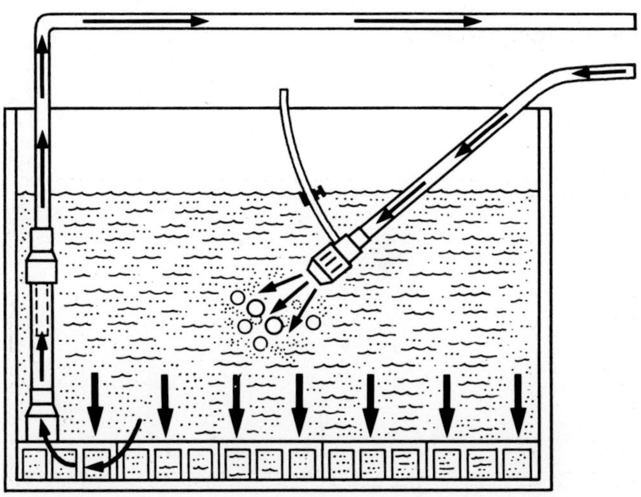

UNDERGRAVEL (U/G) OR SUB-GRAVEL FILTERS

These filters, as their name suggests, are placed on the floor of the aquarium, and are covered with gravel to a minimum depth of 7.5 cm (3 in). The gravel acts as the filter medium in this case, so must be relatively coarse (approximately 3 mm [$^{1}/_{8}$ in]), to ensure that it does not block the filter's pores. Debris is drawn down with water by means of an air pump, through the gravel, where it is degraded by bacteria. For maximum effectiveness, the filter plate should cover the whole of the floor of the aquarium. These filters are produced in standard sizes, but some can be cut to fit any size of tank.

Undergravel filters are relatively unobtrusive compared to other systems, and inexpensive. The air

The nitrogen cycle:
Nitrite is a nitrogen compound which is formed in the aquarium by the breakdown of organic substances, such as fish faeces, urine, food remains and the dead parts of plants. Nitrite is only one of the stages in the breakdown of organic nitrogen to inorganic nitrate.

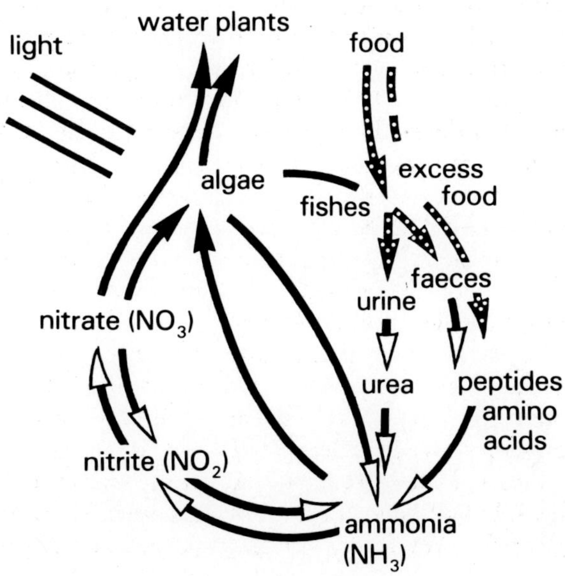

pump must be left on continuously, otherwise the beneficial aerobic bacteria will suffer, and the system will break down. These filters can become overworked, so any accumulated debris on top of the gravel should be siphoned off once a fortnight to lighten the load. Plants can also affect the efficiency of undergravel filters, as their roots may grow down through the pores and block them – also making it harder to thin out the vegetation without disturbing the whole tank. However, you can overcome this problem by growing the plants in plastic pots.

BOX FILTERS

Box filters are a common alternative to the underground filter, or they may be used in conjunction with it. They fall into two categories: fitted outside or inside the tank. Although the latter type take up less space, often fitting in the corner of a tank, they are somewhat harder to service, as will be necessary at regular intervals. Larger tanks certainly benefit from a filter of the external type, which is less restricted in size than its internal counterpart.

The box consists of a perspex container filled with a combination of filter wool, activated carbon in the form of charcoal and, sometimes, gravel. A layer of charcoal is sandwiched between the two layers of nylon wool, with gravel at the bottom to weight down the container. Special wool and carbon are produced for these filters, and should always be used in preference to other similar materials, such as cotton wool, which is not recommended. Bone carbon is used because it sinks in water and is more absorbent than wood carbons. In some cases, filter wool is re-usable, while the carbon can be partially reactivated by heating. It is responsible for removing the toxic substances which are in solution, while the wool takes out solid debris from the water. Acid peat is also occasionally added to box filters, depending on the fish concerned and the state of the water.

These filters require an air pump to operate them, air being introduced through a narrow-bore tube, and exiting through a broader outlet, drawing water out behind it. This in turn causes more water to enter the filter. In an external filter, water is drawn up out of the tank, through the filter bed, and is then returned to the tank.

Left External filter worked by an air-lift. **Right** Air-lift system shown in detail.

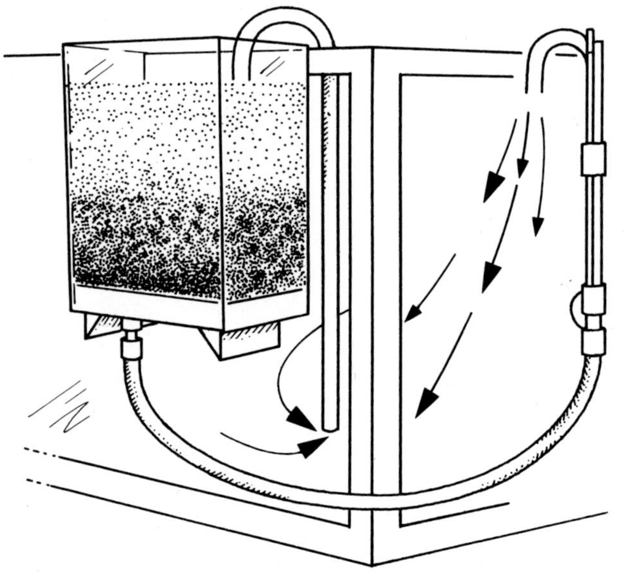

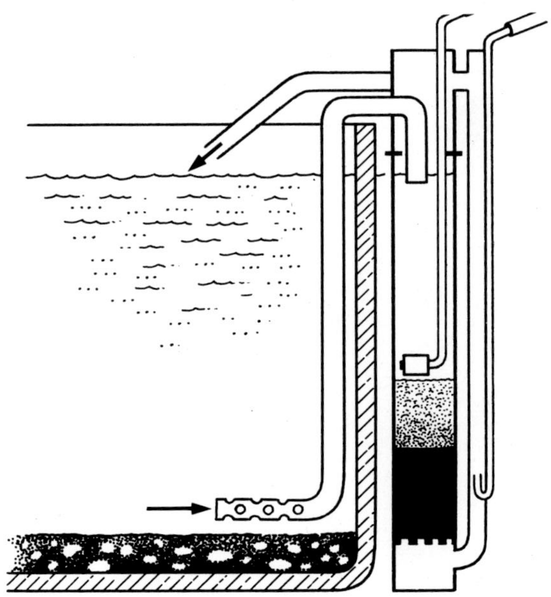

RECENT DEVELOPMENTS IN FILTER TECHNOLOGY

Two recent innovations in filter technology are the poly-foam and power models. The poly-foam filter fits inside the tank. It acts like a sponge, serving as a mechanical filter, and a population of aerobic bacteria will develop on it. When soiled, it is washed off in warm water. Unlike power filters, poly-foam units must be connected to an air pump. In the case of the power filter, part of the unit itself, known as the impeller, is responsible for sucking in water through slits. The water is then passed out through a hole at the top of the filter. This is positioned at surface level, to assist aeration. The filter medium in a power filter can be either a foam sponge or the standard wool-carbon combination. Although relatively expensive, power filters are especially useful for the bigger, messier fish, such as some cichlids.

Further improvement of the water for the fish can be achieved by fitting the Overhead Trickle Purification (OTP) System, designed by King British. This new product has been highly acclaimed since it first became available during 1983. It is not an independent filtraton system, however, but needs to be used in conjunction with a tank filter. The unit, powered by a small air pump, fits into the hood of the aquarium and has a biological mode of action, the water running through a sedimentary rock bed. This helps to increase the oxygen content of the water, and stimulates the growth of beneficial bacteria in the tank itself as a result, while reducing the levels of carbon dioxide and other potentially harmful gases present in solution. The OTP system is of particular value for more delicate fish, such as Discus and Hatchetfish, and can normally be positioned without any modification to the lighting.

Internal filter with renewable cartridge.

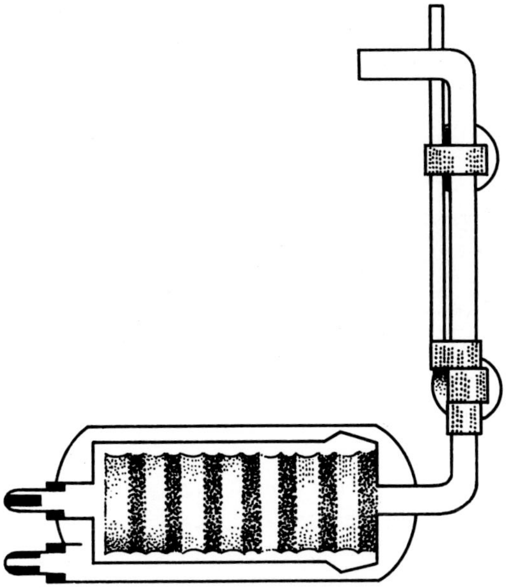

2 PREPARING THE AQUARIUM FOR FISH

You should choose the tank's position in a room with great care. The site should be out of direct sunlight, because the aquarium's appearance will soon be spoilt by the resulting excessive algal growth, and the heat of the sun's rays is likely to affect the temperature of the water. Sudden changes of this nature will be harmful to the fish. For the same reason, tanks should never be placed in close proximity to room heaters, or near doors or windows where the temperature might fluctuate significantly. The background itself is not vital, because you can buy scenic sheets which fit the back of the tank. You will need a power point within easy reach of the tank, and you should make sure the site is sufficiently accessible for maintenance purposes. Tanks positioned at eye-level are difficult to service.

When you have bought a new tank, wash it out thoroughly with salt water, and wipe it carefully at the same time with a clean cloth, just in case there are any minute slivers of glass present which could subsequently lodge, to ill-effect, in a fish's gills. Do not use detergents or disinfectants, as these are likely to prove toxic if any residues still remain after rinsing the tank out with cold water.

Once a large tank is full, it will be impossible to move without removing the water; one litre of water weighs approximately 0.8 kg (1 gal of water weighs just over 8 lb). It is therefore vital that you choose a secure base for the tank; and whether or not a stand is used, place a layer of polystyrene under the tank itself. This serves to counteract any unevenness in the surface that it is standing on, which would result in additional pressure being put on the glass of the tank, possibly causing it to leak.

THE FLOOR COVERING

Aquarium gravel is the most common choice for the floor of the tank. A coarse grade, with individual particles of about 3–4 mm (⅛ in), should be selected, especially when an undergravel filter is to be used. River sand is used in some tanks, but fine sand is not generally recommended, as the water will not be able to circulate effectively between the granules. Also, plant roots will have difficulty penetrating a solid mass of sand.

When setting up a tank, the amount of gravel required can be calculated roughly on a basis of 1 kg per 4.5 l (2 lb per gal) of water. Artificially-coloured gravel is popular, and available in an array of colours, but it is important to ensure that the dyeing agent remains fast in water. Although gravel obtained from aquarist shops has often been washed already, you should wash it again to remove any remaining debris, and treat it to ensure that no parasites or other harmful organisms are introduced into the tank with it.

Washing is simply and effectively carried out using a plastic colander, with holes of a suitable size to retain the gravel or sand. Then transfer the gravel to a plastic bucket containing a solution of potassium permanganate (obtainable from a pharmacist). Stir the gravel thoroughly several times over the course of a couple of days, and then wash it again until the water is clear of any purple tinge. Although such treatment involves extra work, it is considerably easier to eliminate potential problems at this stage, rather than when the tank has been set up and the fish introduced.

THE ADVANTAGES OF LIVING PLANTS

Although plastic plants are now available, and look extremely realistic in some cases, the provision of living plants in the aquarium will undoubtedly help to maintain the biological balance of the environment. They utilize the nitrate produced from the breakdown of waste products by bacteria, and are also involved in gas exchange, carrying out a process known as photosynthesis.

During the day, plants take up carbon dioxide from the water, which, in the presence of light, is used to produce carbohydrates for food, and in return they give off oxygen to the tank. At night, however, photosynthesis ceases and the situation is reversed, the plants utilizing oxygen in minute quantities and releasing carbon dioxide. Some plants are better oxygenators than others, and this feature is directly related to the surface area of the their leaves. Those with many small leaves, such as Java Moss, are better in this respect than broad-leaved species. The role of plants in maintaining a healthy aquatic environment was appreciated as long ago as 1850, when Robert Warrington gave details to the Chemical Society of how he was able to maintain goldfish in tanks without changing the water over several months if living plants were included from the outset.

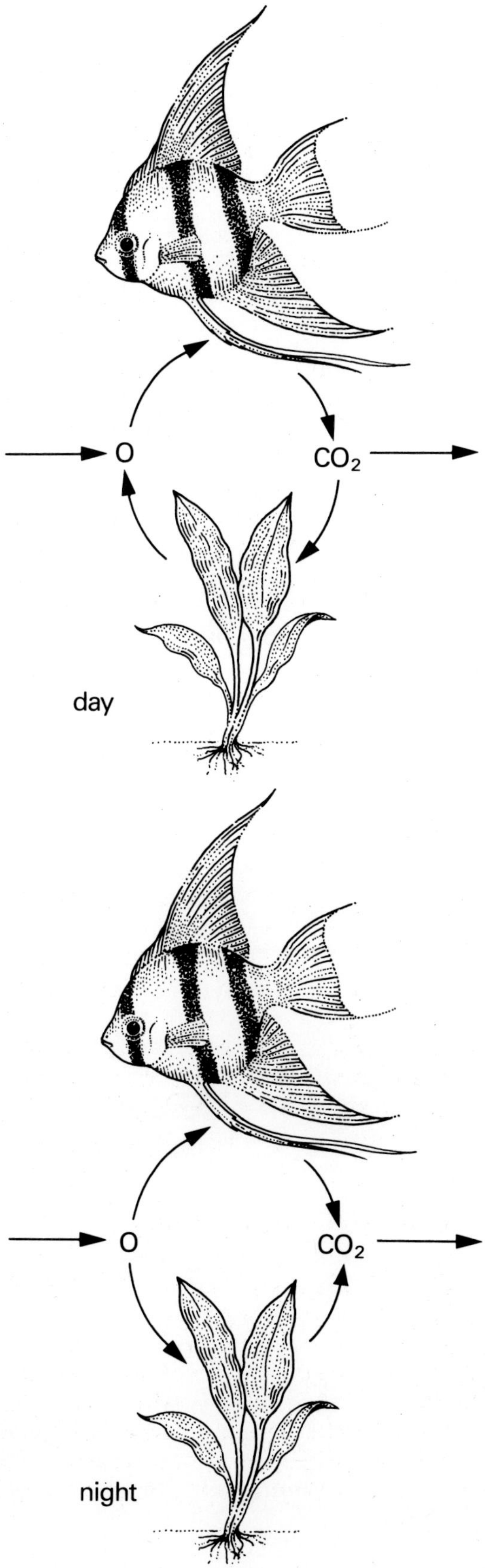

Gaseous exchange between water, plants and fish.

Jarva Moss (*Vesicularia dubyana*) is a good oxygenator in a tank.

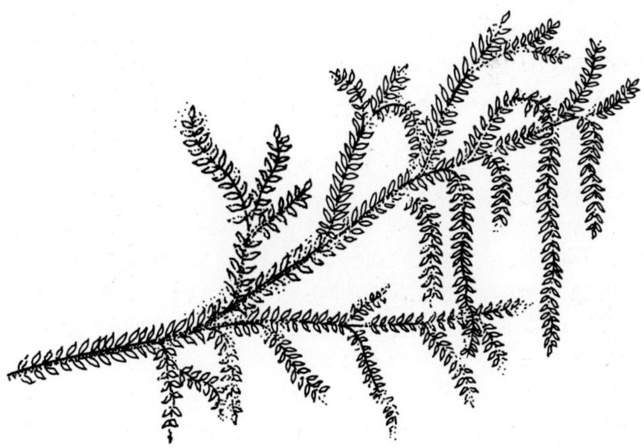

THE CHOICE OF PLANTS

A very wide range of plants is available for the aquarium, and these may be sold either individually, or as mixed collections for various sizes of tank. It is important to have some details about a particular type of plant before acquiring it, so that its suitability for, and place in, the tank can be assessed in advance.

Jack Dempsey Cichlid (*Cichlasoma octofasciatum*). This fish is destructive towards vegetation.

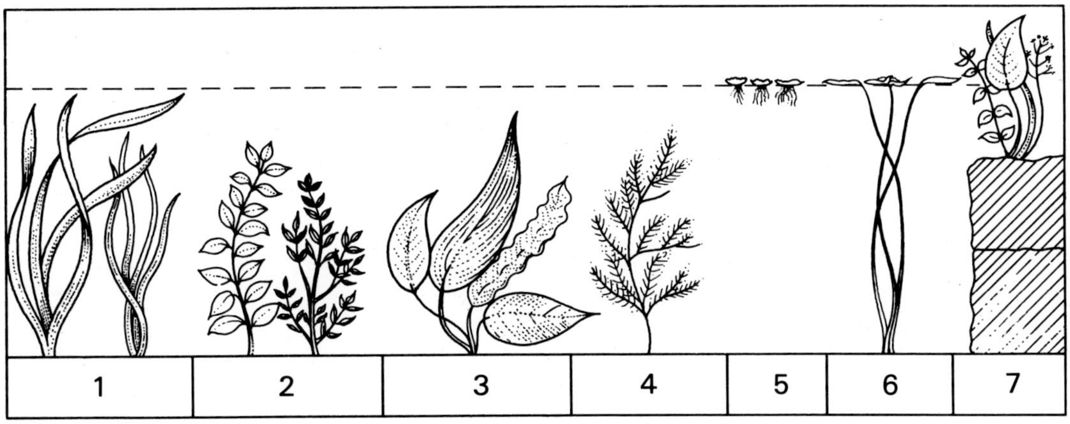

Water-plant types:
1 with strap-like leaves; **2** with coarse or mossy leaves; **3** with long stalks; **4** with feathery leaves; **5** floating plants; **6** rooted plants with floating leaves; **7** marsh plants.

Indeed, not all plants offered would normally be totally submerged throughout the year. Many cryptocornes, or 'crypts', of which over fifty-five species are recognized, are marshland plants. They are totally immersed in water during the wet season only, for two months or so out of the whole year. Members of this genus are confined to south-east Asia. They are relatively slow-growing in the aquarium, and in the natural state remain inactive when submerged. The various species occur in several colours, ranging from bluish-green in the case of *Cryptocorne affinis* to reddish in some strains of *C. wendtii*. One of the smaller members of the group is *C. nevillii*, which reaches a size of about 7.5 cm (3 in), whereas *C. ciliata* can grow to 60 cm (2 ft), making it rather large for the average aquarium.

Successful cultivation of cryptocornes requires a minimum of disturbance, and moving them will prove a definite set-back to their growth. They tend not to like excessive light, or hard water, but adapt well to the temperature of a tropical tank, providing it does not exceed 27°C (80°F). Flowering is rare, although *C. griffithii* is most likely to yield results in this direction.

The genus *Echinodorus* contains the aquarium plants which are often known as 'Amazon Sword Plants'. Although the majority of species occur in Central and South America, others are known from the Caribbean, as well as Europe and North Africa. Those commonly sold as aquarium plants range in size from about 7.5 cm (3 in) in the case of *E. tenellus* to about 40 cm (16 in) for *E. bleheri*. Although many have elongated leaves, those of *E. cordifolius* are heart-shaped. Water which is relatively soft suits *Echinodorus* well, and these plants are easily propagated by means of their runners, or from small plantlets which develop on the stems. They are very suitable for tanks where the fish have a tendency to destroy vegetation, because their tough fronds offer good protection, and they are fast-growing by nature.

Another strong plant, which is also extremely adaptable, thriving even in coldwater aquaria, is *Elodea densa*. It is widely available, and soon roots readily from cuttings. *Elodea* thrives especially in well-lit surroundings in hard water and so is not really compatible with the various cryptocornes. *Elodea*, with its high lime requirement, may actually serve to soften hard water. Two other forms, *E. canadensis* (Canadian pondweed) and *E. callitrichoides* (Chilean pondweed), should be used only in coldwater surroundings, as they will not adapt well to the warmth of a tropical tank.

Hygrophyla polysperma, a native of India, is a highly versatile plant unaffected by the condition of the water. It can adjust to temperatures ranging from 12°–30°C (54°–86°F) and parts are easily rooted. Planted in bunches, it shows to good effect against darker *Cryptocoryne* species and, once established, provides ample cover for the fish. *H. difformis* is a more demanding member of the genus, preferring soft water and good light.

Ludwigia natans also appreciates bright surroundings, but does not thrive in tanks where the water temperature is much above 25°C (77°F). Cuttings grow readily and may be required if the lower leaves are lost, often as a result of inadequate light. *Myriophyllum*, which has much finer leaves, is very similar to *Ludwigia* in its requirements. *Nomaphila stricta* also does well in good light, but can stand a higher range of temperatures, between 22°–30°C (72°–86°F). It grows relatively fast under suitable conditions, but often proves a favourite food with any snails present in the tank.

Various members of the genus *Sagittaria* are used to decorate aquaria, and out of these, *S. latifola* is perhaps most commonly seen. *Sagittaria* does well across a fairly broad temperature range, and will not require excessive lighting. Light exposure can, however, affect the colour of these plants, as is also the case with members of other genera. *S. subulata*, for example, becomes reddish when exposed to a high density of illumination.

Vallisneria, which has a similar appearance to certain *Sagittaria* is often found in planted aquaria, located towards the back of the tank. *V. spiralis* can reach a size of 60 cm (2 ft), and the subspecies *V. s.torta* has more twisted leaves than the nominate race. The giant form, *V. gigantea*, should only be acquired for large and deep set-ups, as its leaves are likely to grow to at least 1 m (3 ft) in length. Distinct male and female plants of this species are recognized.

FLOATING PLANTS

While the plants discussed previously live rooted in the substrate of the tank, there is another group which naturally occur on the surface of the water, giving areas of shade beneath them. The Underwater Banana Plant (*Nymphoides aquatica*), named after its tuberous roots, which resemble a cluster of the fruit, can either be allowed to float freely, or be planted in the substrate. It prefers slightly acid water, but, in common with all members of this group, if the conditions are too favourable, its foliage may completely smother the surface of the tank, unless it is held in check.

The attractive Water Sprite prefers an uncovered tank. The form known as *Ceratopteris cornuta* can grow to a size of 50 cm (20 in) if given adequate space in relatively soft water with a temperature between 20° and 30°C (68°–86°F). Its dangling roots are a favourite retreat of young fry. Another species, *C. thalictroides*, known as Sumatra Fern, is also quite often available.

Salvinia auriculata is more suitable for the smaller tropical tank, by virtue of its size, with leaves only about 1.25 cm ($\frac{1}{2}$ in) long. It is a rootless fern which thrives in a well-lit environment, and is favoured by bubble-nest builders, including the Fighting Fish, to lend support to their nests. Although *Salvinia* produces spores, these do not mature in the aquarium, and

Cryptocoryne affinis.

Ludwigia natans.

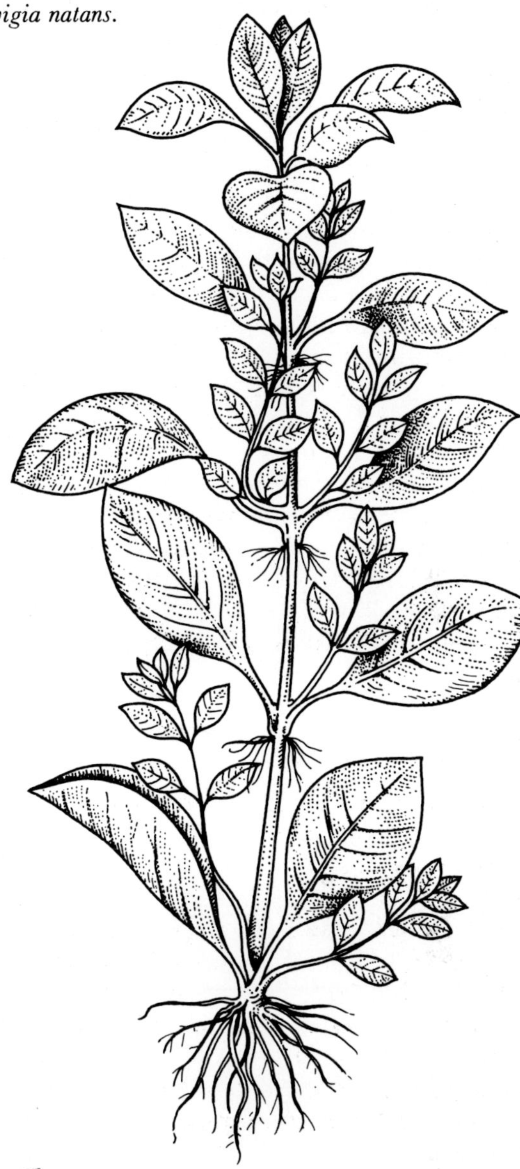

Nymphoides aquatica.

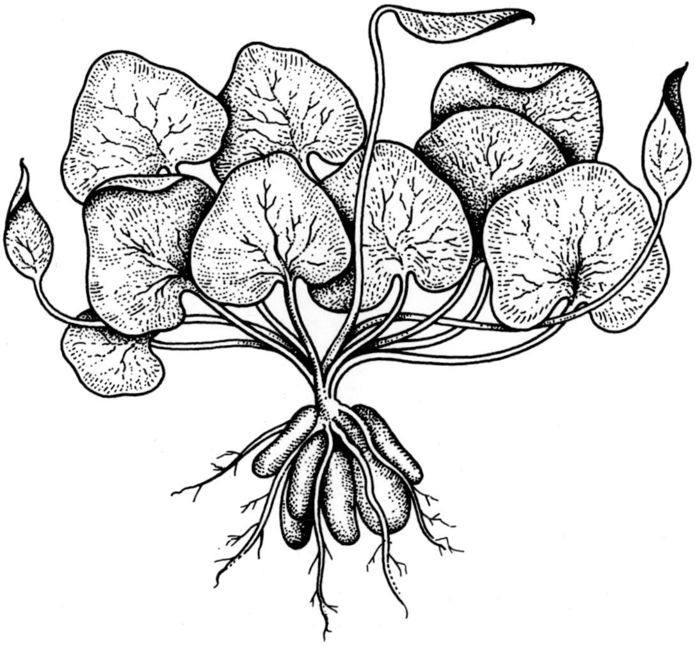

Elodea densa. Plants such as this can be bought as cuttings and anchored into the substrate, where they will take root.

spread occurs by pieces breaking off from the main plant. Another small tropical American floating plant often seen in aquaria is *Limnobium stoloniferum* which requires soft water conditions. Propagation in this case is from runners.

SUMMARY

This section has dealt with a selection of the most commonly available and easily-grown aquatic plants; it is not a comprehensive review of this aspect of the

Echinodorus cordifolius.

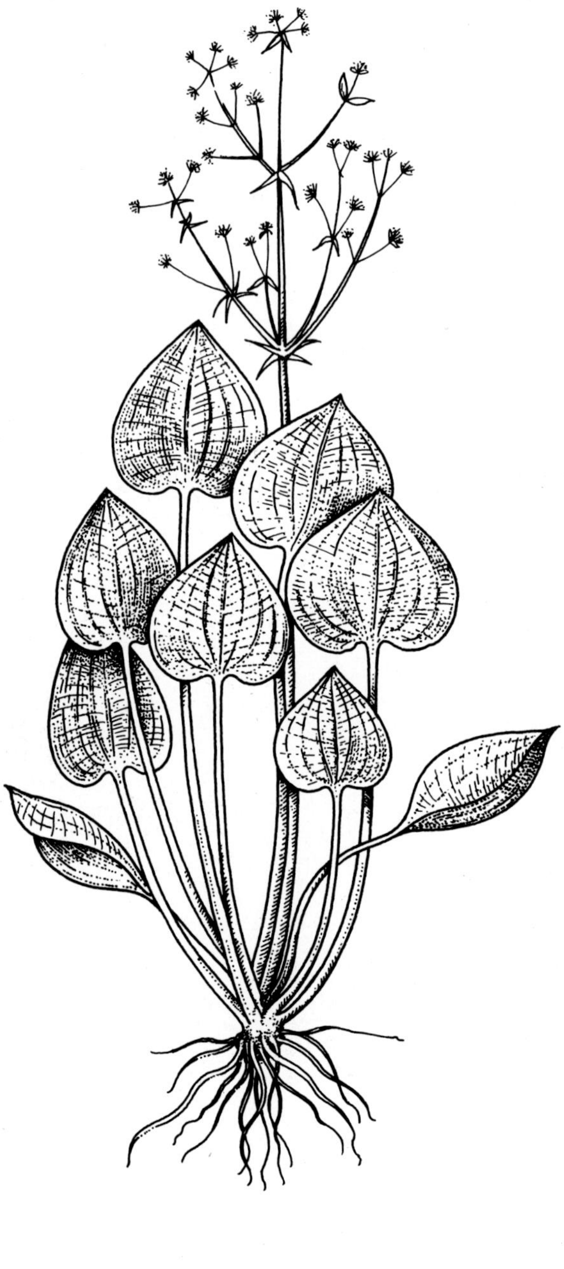

Vallisneria spiralis.

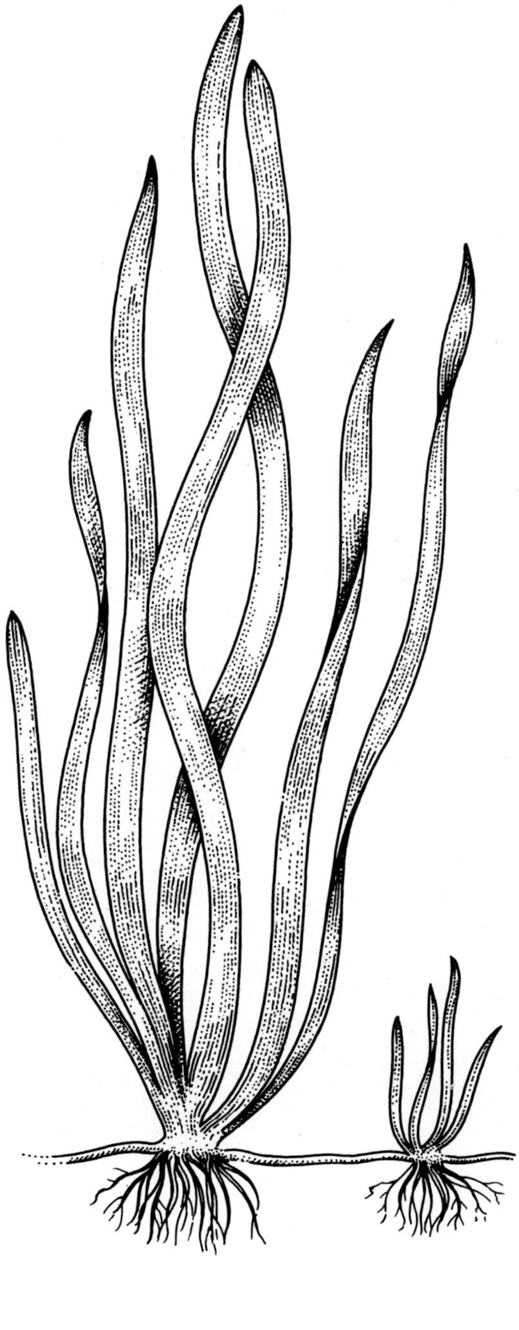

hobby. There are now several books available which are devoted solely to the topic of aquarium plants, and you should refer to these for detailed information on a particular species. In addition, there are specialist aquatic nurseries that sell a wide range of water plants, and give advice on their subsequent care. Such nurseries often advertise in fish-keeping journals, and generally operate a mail-order business, as well as catering for callers.

PLANTING PRINCIPLES

You should work out an overall plan for the tank, including rockwork as well as plants. Taller plants such as *Vallisneria* and *Sagittaria* should be placed towards the back of the tank, and a Sword Plant should be positioned in the centre. Smaller plants such as *C. nevilli* are put in the foreground.

When you have bought the plants, you should wash them off thoroughly in a salt solution, because they can introduce pests such as *Planaria* into the aquarium. A solution made up with 31 g (1 oz) of salt

Poecilobrycon unifasciatus, like all pencilfish, can be kept in a tank with dense marginal vegetation and some roots to provide cover.

Acanthopsis choirorhynchus, a large species of roach, which is active at night, and digs vigorously in the substrate, sometimes bringing up plants that are too small or insufficiently rooted.

Haplochromis euchilus. A cichlid which uses its thick lips to strip algae off rocks.

per 4.5 l (1 gal) of water will be adequate for this purpose. Then rinse them off and remove any dead leaves before placing them in the tank.

The floor covering of the tank is not as significant for plants as may be thought. Those which are genuinely adapted for life in water take most of their nutrients directly from their aquatic environment, and not via their roots, which merely provide anchorage in the substrate. Many different planting media are recommended for different plants, but the majority of plants prove fairly adaptable. You can plant them all individually in small pots, to cater for their individual preferences, but this may detract from the overall appearance of the aquarium, and is not strictly necessary. However, pots are an advantage in a tank where the occupants are likely to uproot vegetation. In addition the root system, and thus the growth, of plants such as cryptocornes will not be damaged by later movement if they are set in pots. A mixture of loam and acid peat, covered with the aquarium substrate, should be used in such pots.

PLASTIC PLANTS

It is not always possible to establish living plants in the aquarium, especially when the tank houses fish such as Jack Dempsey Cichlids, which will destroy vegetation. Plastic plants do have certain advantages over their living counterparts. They are not likely to introduce disease to the tank, and there are no problems in establishing them. Their plastic foliage does not deteriorate and thus detract from the overall appearance of the tank, yet like genuine plants, they provide cover for the fish. The problem of blue-green algae developing in the tank is more likely to arise with plastic plants, however, because excess nitrate, which would normally be utilized by other aquatic vegetation, will be circulating in the water.

ROCKWORK

In the same way that plants provide cover, food and breeding habitats, so rockwork in the tank can also benefit the fish. Some cichlids may be induced to breed with the presence of flat stones or sunken flowerpots, while certain catfish, for example, will feed on algae growing on rockwork, and often hide beneath it. Only hard, non-soluble rocks, such as granite, slate or sandstone, should be included in the tank, however, because they will not affect the water's hardness. Limestone rocks contain calcium carbonate, which will slowly dissolve into the water in the presence of dissolved carbon dioxide, causing the water to increase significantly in hardness. This will prove detrimental to the vast majority of fish and plants.

Although you can buy aquarium stone, it is possible to collect suitable rocks from many places, such as river beds. If you're in doubt as to whether a particular rock contains limestone, there is a simple test that you can carry out to detect the presence of this chemical. Carefully apply a few drops of hydrochloric or sulphuric acid to the rock's surface; any sign of effervescence indicates the presence of calcium carbonate. Rockwork intended for the aquarium should be scrubbed off thoroughly in salt water, and rinsed before being placed in the tank.

WOOD

Wood in the aquarium can be decorative, and may form a significant feature of spawning tanks. Willow root, for example, can often be used to induce members of the genus *Aphyosemion* to spawn, the eggs of these tooth-carp being laid in amongst the individual strands. Alder, birch or oak are also suitable woods for use in aquaria.

Once again, the first step is to sterilize the wood completely, and this can be done by placing it in an old, large saucepan complete with a lid. The wood should then be boiled for a couple of hours, ensuring that it remains covered with water throughout this period. After a final scrubbing and thorough rinse, it is ready for use in the tank. In Germany, the wood sold as 'Moorkienholz', obtained from sphagnum bogs, is popular with aquarists.

WATER: HARDNESS AND ACIDITY

The relative hardness of water is influenced by its source. Water that contains significant proportions of dissolved calcium and magnesium salts, obtained from the rocks which it has come into contact with, is described as being 'hard'. Rainwater, on the other hand, is relatively pure, being free from such salts, and is therefore referred to as 'soft'. The degree of hardness is measured on the German °DH scale, one unit being equivalent to 10 mg of calcium, in the form of calcium oxide, which is present in 1 l (1.75 pt) of water. Most fish, living in areas of water swollen by rain, prefer relatively soft water, although there are exceptions, such as the Rift Valley cichlids, which occur in the isolated lakes formed in this arid, volcanic region. The following table gives an indication of the constitution of water, based on the °DH scale. Distilled water, being pure, has a zero rating.

°DH	Water
0–4	Very soft
5–8	Soft
9–12	Moderately hard
13–18	Harder
19–30	Hard
30+	Very hard

Note Although the °DH scale is most widely used, there is another system, with a degree being equivalent in this case to 14.3 parts per millilitre (ppm) of calcium carbonate. Conversion entails multiplying °DH by 0.56 to obtain the corresponding figure. These figures can be converted back to °DH by multiplying by 1.785.

Hardness of water can be further sub-divided into permanent and temporary hardness. Permanent hardness results from the presence of sulphates, and unlike temporary hardness, cannot be removed by boiling. Temporary hardness, sometimes expressed as the KH reading, is significant because it can act as a buffer in the water to overcome minor pH changes.

The pH value is a measurement of the relative acidity of the water in the tank. The scale of pH readings can extend from 0 to 14, with 7 being neutral. When below this figure, water conditions are said to be acid, whereas above 7, they are alkaline. Most tapwater varies between 7 and 8, and this is suitable to maintain many fish without additional treatment. Discus and killifish require more acid conditions, however, whereas the Rift Valley cichlids come from alkaline waters. In addition, the pH is often of vital importance for the successful breeding of other fish, such as barbs, which require soft, acid water. The individual requirements of particular groups are considered later, in the section devoted to the fish themselves. All fish are very sensitive to any sudden alterations in the pH value of their surroundings, and a fluctuation of more than one unit in a day is likely to have fatal consequences. However, gradual adaptation over quite a wide range is possible.

TESTING WATER CONDITIONS

When assessing the degree of hardness, or the pH value, of a sample of water, the simplest means is to acquire the appropriate test kits available from aquarist dealers. These are quite straightforward to use, and are often more reliable than other methods, such as litmus paper, used for pH measurements. A local dealer is likely to have similar water conditions, and this may be advantageous when buying fish.

MODIFICATION OF HARDNESS AND pH

On occasions, it may be necessary to adjust these levels for particular fish. If the water is too hard, you add distilled water in the correct proportions to attain the desired degree of softness. For example, knowing that the tap water is 16°DH and aiming to obtain very soft water with a DH reading of 2°, fourteen parts of distilled water must be added to two parts of tap water, as shown. Boiling will remove the carbonate component of hardness, (and also lower the ability of the water to effectively neutralize pH changes, as its buffering capacity is compromised), but this alteration is only temporary, because carbon dioxide dissolved in the water will gradually regenerate the carbonate. The addition of calcium sulphate to the tank will increase the hardness of the water if this is necessary, but such alterations should always be checked over a period of time, before the fish are added to the tank.

Alteration of the °DH of water.

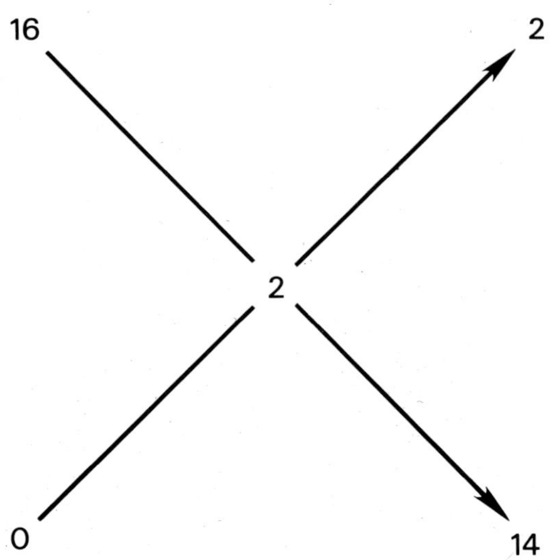

As mentioned previously, limestone rocks in the aquarium will increase the hardness of the water, and they will also raise the pH. The simplest and safest means of lowering the pH value is to add peat to the tank. This is done by including aquarium peat in a box filter, which the water circulates through. Alternatively, peat stitched into a nylon bag and placed in the tank, working on the basis of a handful of peat per 4.5 l (1 gal) of water, will also serve to soften the water over the course of a day or so. The peat will need replacing about every fortnight to maintain its action, usually when the filter itself is changed.

ASSEMBLING THE TANK COMPONENTS

After the tank has been placed in position, and the undergravel filter added, if one is to be used, the gravel can be tipped carefully into the aquarium. This should slope down towards the front so that subsequently any debris will be evident. The thicker layer of gravel at the back of the tank also provides a deeper substrate for plant roots, and serves to partially disguise pots if these are used.

It is preferable to fill the tank at least half-full of water before putting the plants and other tank decorations in place. Water from a cold tap is safer, because in some cases the concentration of copper, dissolved from pipes in the heating system into the water, may poison the fish. If the water is poured carefully on to a plate located on the surface of the gravel, it should not disturb the actual gravel base.

Then, working to your plan, you can set the plants in position, starting at the back of the tank. Planting tools are available to make this easier. Plants with long roots, such as *Cryftocoryne* and *Vallisneria* species, must be planted in a correspondingly deep hole. As with all rooted plants, these must be set with their crowns above the substrate, thus ensuring that they do not rot once they are in place. Spacing between individual plants depends on the type concerned. A minimum area of 5 sq cm (2 sq in) should be allowed, with a gap of 15 cm (6 in) separating plants which reach a larger size. Cuttings are often planted in small groups, each weighed down individually with a suitable stone, until they have rooted. It is very important that the plants are kept moist after purchase until they are back in water, because their leaves may otherwise be damaged by desiccation, and their appearance subsequently spoilt.

Rocks and wood can then be added, taking care to leave a sufficient swimming area for the fish themselves. The rockwork must be firm, especially in tanks for larger fish, such as Oscars, because they may dislodge unstable rocks with serious consequences, and also injure themselves on any rough, exposed edges. If wood is used, it must remain saturated to keep it below the water level; it should not float on the surface. This can be achieved by wedging it soundly with rockwork. It is also possible to encourage vegetation to develop on the wood. A plant which looks most attractive when growing on sunken wood or roots is Java Fern (*Microsorium pteropus*).

Microsorium pteropus.

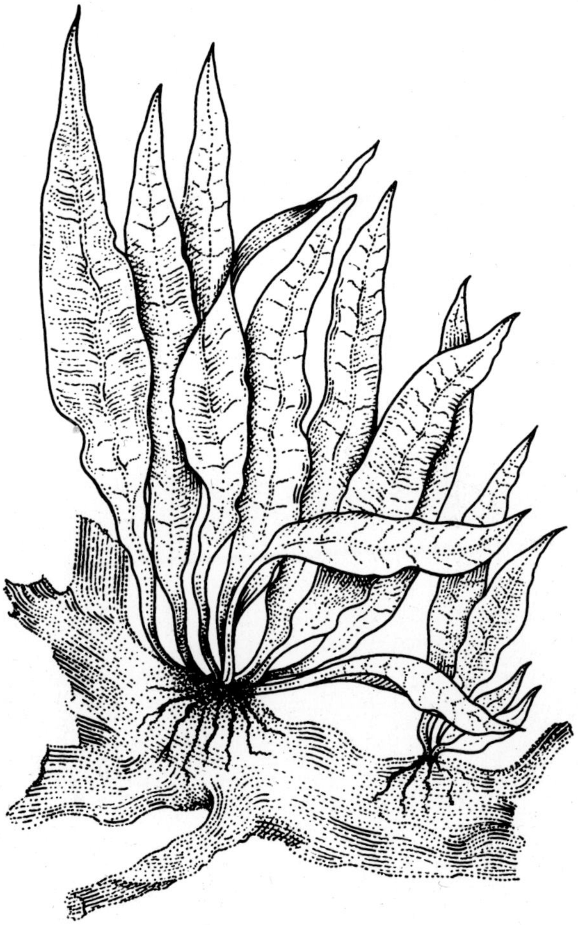

THE ELECTRICAL APPARATUS

Next, the electrical components of the aquarium can be wired up and placed in position. If in any doubt about the wiring, you should seek advice from a qualified electrician. It is possible to use a junction box for the wiring so that all the units feed into the mains supply via a single plug, which is safer and also dispenses with the need for adaptors. When using a combined heater and thermostat, the unit should be fixed onto the back of the tank by its rubber suckers, keeping the thermostat higher than the heating unit, so that it is not positioned horizontally. Under no circumstances should such units be switched on out of the water or buried in the substrate. An independent thermostat must always be placed as far away as possible from the heater, preferably at the other end of the tank, with the thermometer placed close to the thermostat on the front panel where it can be easily read.

The air pump will need to be included in the circuitry, and fixed in with the filter and airstone as appropriate. The system can then be tested, and the water left to warm up, which is likely to take several hours. Various alarm systems are now available to detect any electrical failures in the heating system, and it is worth adding one of these to the tropical tank.

TOXIC CHEMICALS IN SOLUTION

You cannot add the fish to the tank immediately the water temperature has stabilized at the desired level, because the level of chlorine present in the tap water will poison them. As little as 0.1 mg of chlorine per litre (1.75 gal) has proved toxic for fish. Leave the water to stand for at least twenty-four hours to enable the gas to come out of solution. However, aquarium dechlorinators are available for emergencies. These, used as directed, speed up this process considerably, so the water should be safe for the fish within an hour or so of adding the treatment. Although fluoride is also mixed in some water supplies to assist with dental health care, the concentration used is not likely to be harmful to fish, and at any rate this chemical will be neutralized along with the chlorine.

A compound that is produced from waste products in the newly established tank, and which is likely to be detrimental to the fishes' health, however, is ammonia. At this stage, there are no bacteria established to break it down to relatively harmless nitrate. Zeolite, which is produced from natural resin, and sold in sachets, is now available to help overcome this problem. The sachets fit into the filtration system or in the tank itself. This compound effectively absorbs ammonia from the water, and can be re-used repeatedly by immersing it overnight in a cup of salt water.

INTRODUCING THE FISH

If possible, the aquarium should be set up at least a week before any fish are acquired. This will give the plants an opportunity to become established. It is preferable to purchase all the fish for the tank simultaneously, from the same source. The addition of new arrivals to an established tank can lead to problems such as bullying. Fish are usually sold in plastic bags, containing a relatively small amount of their tank water, but a large volume of air to ensure that they have sufficient oxygen for their journey. This is why a dealer often blows up the bag before sealing it: contrary to popular belief, our lungs extract only a proportion of the atmospheric oxygen inhaled, a significant quantity being exhaled again at the end of each breath.

The temperature of the water in the bag will fall during transit, and once at home, the bag should be floated in the tank water for a period of time to enable the water temperatures to even out, before releasing the fish. This gives them an opportunity to adjust gradually to the fluctuations in temperature which they have experienced, and thus reduces the stress on them. The bag can then be gently inverted into the water, allowing the fish out into their new environment.

The fish will take a while to adjust to their move, and should be watched closely for any signs of illness, which is especially likely to develop at this stage. Some, such as Dwarf Rainbow Cichlids (*Pelamatochromis kribensis*), may undergo a loss of colour at first, but this is only a temporary change.

SNAILS

Some aquarists favour the presence of snails in aquaria, pointing out that they will consume algae and other debris which otherwise would accumulate in the tank. The opposite view regards snails not as beneficial, but as potential sources of problems, citing the damage caused to growing vegetation and further soiling of the tank as examples. Undeniably, though, snails do provide another focus of interest in the aquarium and can reproduce successfully therein.

However, young snails often fall victims to carnivorous fish, so a population explosion is unlikely to occur, as their numbers will be kept in check naturally.

Apple snails belonging to the genus *Ampullaria* have unusual breeding habits. They lay their eggs above the water surface, and the eggs must be kept moist if they are to hatch successfully. This can be achieved by positioning an air-stone close by, which gives them a light spray, but prevents them from becoming saturated. The Mystery Snail (*A. cuprina*) is the most desirable member of the genus for the aquarist because it will not destroy vegetation to the same extent as other Apple snails. They feed on a range of items ranging from algae to tubifex.

Ramshorn snails (*Planorbis* species) have a distinctly flat, coiled appearance, and are sometimes introduced accidentally on vegetation. The Red form (*P. corneus*) is often seen in tropical aquaria, but care should be taken to exclude these snails from breeding tanks, because they will consume fish eggs. Ramshorn snails are smaller than Apple snails, the Red species attaining a maximum size of about 1.25 cm ($\frac{1}{2}$ in).

Four snails commonly seen in aquaria:
1 Ramshorn snail;
2 Malayan pond snail;
3 *Ampullaria* with proboscis extended;
4 *Limnaea*, which can be destructive in a planted aquarium.

2

1

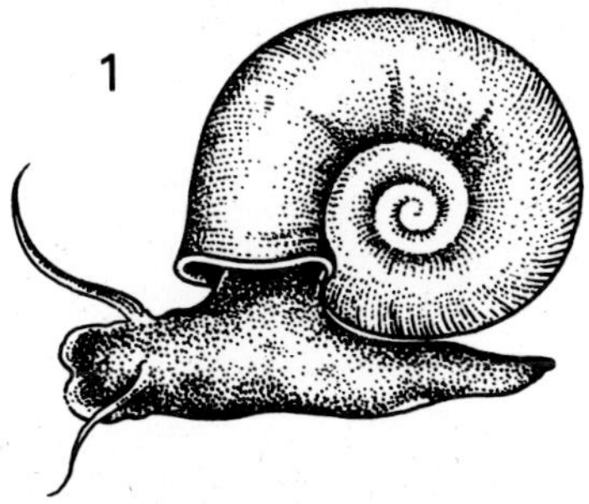

3

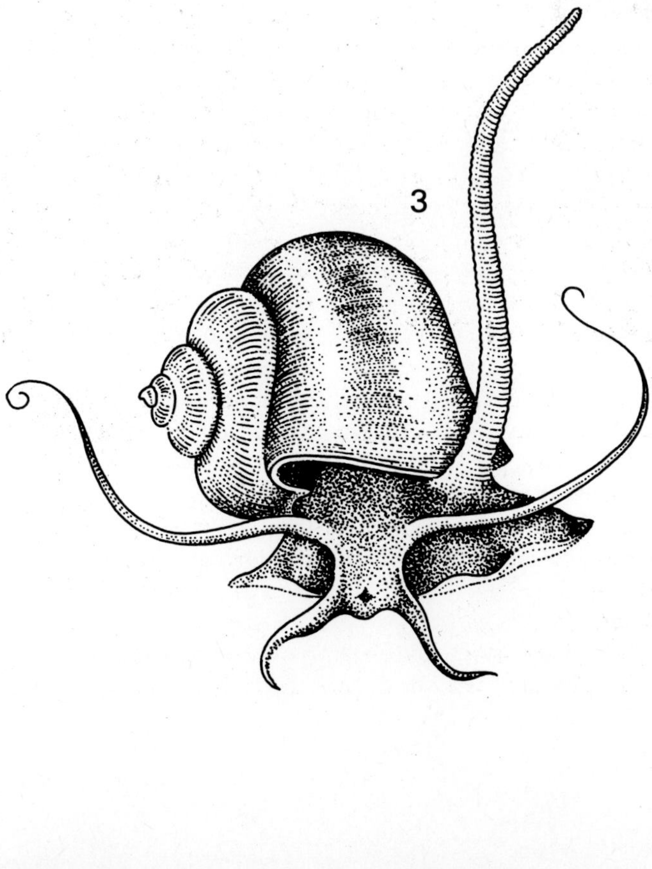

4

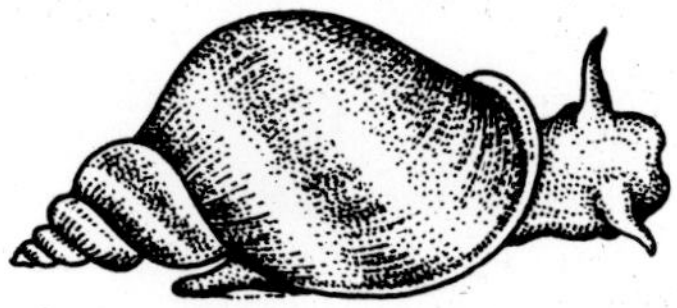

Certain snails, such as the Japanese Live-bearing snail (*Viviparus malleatus*), are more suited to a cold water environment. This mollusc, as its name suggests, gives birth to live offspring, and will not damage plants in the aquarium. By contrast, *Limnaea* species can become pests in a planted tank, although it may be possible to overcome their destructive habits to some extent by adding supplementary food, such as well-washed lettuce leaves, weighted down on the floor of the aquarium. *Limnaea* snails can be useful, however, because they will remove *Hydra* from a tank.

Poecilobrycon harrisoni, a form of pencilfish. All pencilfish should be fed as much as possible on live-food.

3 FEEDING AND GENERAL CARE

In the wild, fish eat a range of foods, and their diet is often influenced by seasonal availability. The Bermuda Angelfish (*Holacanthus bermudensis*), for example, feeds largely on plant matter during the winter and spring, becoming carnivorous in the summer. Certain species are adapted to feed on particular foods. In Lake Victoria, where over 170 different species of cichlid occur, some strip algae off rocks using their chisel-like teeth, whereas others, with a wide gape, are predatory in their feeding habits. A few fish, for example some South American characoids, consume the scales of neighbouring fish.

Feeding fish in the aquarium is not difficult, and there is now a wide range of prepared foods available, containing all the ingredients necessary to keep the fish in good health. There is also no risk of introducing disease to the tank occupants using such foods. Most ranges contain a basic staple diet, which can be augmented with other products, such as conditioning food. It is preferable to select one brand, and use the various items of the range as recommended. Colour foods, to improve the coloration of certain fish, such as Flame Tetras (*Hyphessobrycon flammeus*), are also now available, as are diets specifically intended for fry and particular fish such as guppies.

Basic diets are manufactured in the form of flakes and tablets, which contain very little water compared to natural foods. Certain fish, such as discus and angelfish, can be tamed sufficiently to eat out of the hand, especially when feeding takes place at regular times each day.

It is vital that fish are offered only a relatively small amount of food, which they should consume within minutes of being placed in the tank. One of the most common errors of the novice aquarist is to overfeed the fish. Excess food will pollute the tank, and may harm the fish. Their digestive systems are not adapted to eating one large meal daily; in the wild, they feed throughout the day. Several small meals are therefore recommended, the food being introduced in a feeding ring, which floats on the surface, thus retaining the flakes in one place. Flake food will sink slowly, and will then be consumed by bottom-feeders, such as barbs and catfish. Tablet diets are more commonly used for such fish; they can nibble pieces off a block.

Haplochromis polystigma. One of the predatory cichlids, certainly not recommended for inclusion in any community tank.

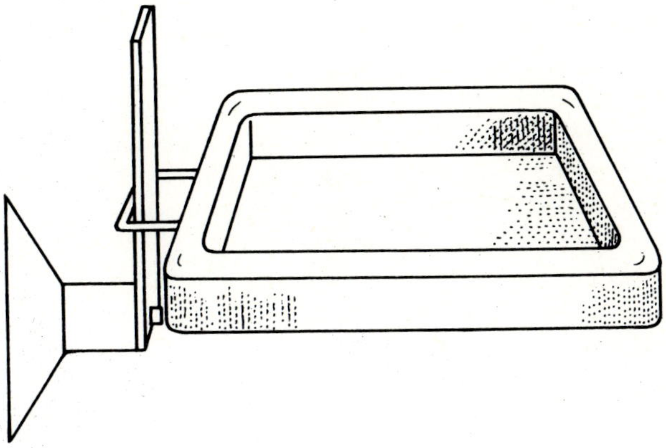

Feeding ring.

LIVEFOODS

Livefoods fed to fish can be divided into two categories: those invertebrates which occur naturally in water; and those which are cultivated or collected from other environments. Although fish undoubtedly appreciate such items on their menu, aquatic livefoods present a potential health hazard, as a range of other creatures, as well as disease, may be accidentally introduced with them. Aquatic beetles, for example, will attack all fish, and *Hydra*, which is related to the jellyfishes, can destroy large numbers of fry in a short period of time by means of its stinging tentacles. Furthermore, *Hydra* may at first sight be confused with *Cyclops*, which is a crustacean actually used as livefood for fish. These two creatures can be distinguished by their movements, as *Cyclops* swims whereas *Hydra*, with its flexible body, contracts down to escape detection at a hint of danger.

Two of the most popular aquatic livefoods for fish are *Daphnia*, also known as water fleas, and *Tubifex* worms; both of which are commonly stocked by aquarist shops. Daphnia are sold in plastic bags full of water, and before purchasing them, a check should be made to ensure that a significant proportion are alive and moving. In any bag, a number will be dead, and if not used immediately, the bag should be kept cool to avoid larger losses. These crustaceans are not, in fact, related to fleas, but have a similar shape and jerky motion.

When feeding daphnia to fish, a special set of sieves should be acquired so that the water can be filtered off from the bag. This helps to reduce the risk of introducing pests present in the water, as they may be more visible in the sieve; but more significantly, if you pour the water containing the daphnia into the tank, it will certainly upset the temperature, and perhaps the pH and °DH values of the water as well. As a source of livefood, daphnia are said to improve colour as well as having a laxative effect on the fish.

Tubifex worms are found in fairly unsavoury surroundings, typically in the vicinity of sewage outlets, where they feed on the effluent. In London, tubifex occur right in the centre of the city, down river in the Thames from Chelsea, and their collection is licensed by the Port of London Authority. Thorough cleansing through running water decreases contamination subsequently, but some aquarists are very doubtful about using tubificid worms for their fish.

The worms can be kept alive for a period of time out of water, with measured quantities usually being sold wrapped in paper. On arrival home, transfer them to a container positioned under a dripping tap, to ensure a constant flow of water over them. They will soon die if left in a jam jar covered in water, unless the water is changed very frequently. Tubifex should be offered to the fish in a special feeder, which is shaped like a nozzle, and prevents the whole mass from sinking to the bottom of the tank at once.

There are various other aquatic livefoods which can be fed to fish, such as gnat larvae found during the summer months in stagnant pools and waterways. The safest method of obtaining these is to attract the adult gnats by leaving a clean bucket, containing aged tap water, outside. They will then lay their eggs, and once the larvae hatch, these can be collected by sieving.

Catfish, such as the Leopard Corydoras (*Corydoras julii*) shown here, often feed near the bottom of a tank.

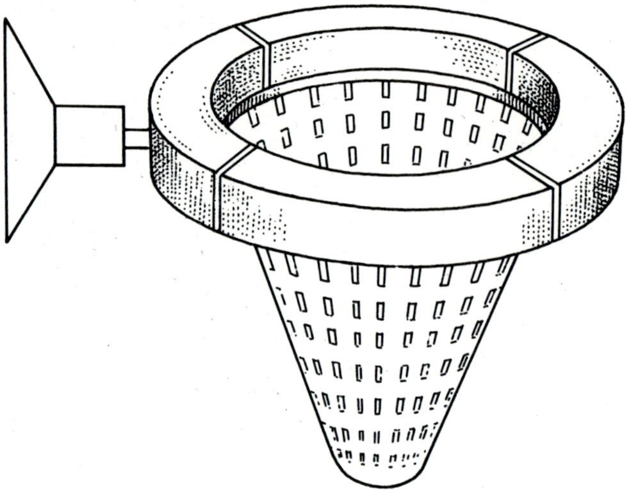

Tubifex worm feeder.

NON-AQUATIC LIVEFOOD

There are always likely to be potential problems over the collection and storage of the previously mentioned invertebrates, and shop supplies are not always reliable. Suitable alternatives can be cultured or obtained with little effort, to overcome such difficulties. Whiteworm (*Enchytraeus*) is typical of this group. A culture is easily established in a disused plastic ice-cream container, half-filled with damp soil, with moistened bread on top. The bread should only be given in relatively small amounts, enough to last the worms for a couple of days, with any surplus then being removed and replaced. On occasions, the bread may have turned red, indicating the presence of a bacterium, *Bacillus prodigiosus*, but this causes no harm. Mites also contaminate some cultures and likewise have no adverse effects on the worms or fish.

The whiteworm culture must be covered with a lid perforated with ventilation holes, to keep it in the dark and to prevent the soil drying out. The soil surface should be sprayed regularly, but it should never be waterlogged. Several colonies can be set up simultaneously using worms purchased from an aquarist dealer, and maintained in cool surroundings, with a temperature between 15° and 20°C (58°–68°F). After a month or so, depending on the conditions, whiteworms can be harvested on a regular basis. They are easily collected from beneath chunks of bread using forceps and can then be washed off and separated from the substrate in a saucer of water, or sieved. The worms range in size from about 0.5–1.25 cm (¼–½ in), and may need to be chopped for feeding to small fish. Specific foods for young fry are considered in the next chapter.

Earthworms are freely available in most gardens, especially during periods of wet weather, when they are drawn to the surface. They are also sold in many angling shops. A worm trap can be set up to avoid digging haphazardly in a garden, by laying damp hessian sacking on a shaded piece of ground, which has been well-watered previously, and then adding some vegetable matter under the sacking to attract the worms. Those found around manure heaps, especially the Brandling, which has a noticeably 'ringed' appearance, should be avoided. After collection, the worms will need to be transferred to a suitable container as for whiteworm, but lined with damp moss and grass, for several days so they can empty their gut contents. Smaller, whole worms are often useful in tempting reticent individuals, such as Siamese Fire Eels (*Mastacembelus erythrotaenia*), to feed when placed directly in front of them. These eels have poor eyesight, and detect food with their nose.

Another commercially available livefood, which has become somewhat more expensive recently, is the Redworm (*Dendrobina rubica*), often used as a fishing bait. These worms can be purchased in pre-packed tubs containing a sterile media, and then fed directly. They tend to be somewhat smaller than earthworms, which is an advantage as they may not need to be cut up for feeding purposes. When kept in a temperature of 5°–10°C (40°–50°F), the supply will last for several weeks, as long as the media is not allowed to dry out.

Fruit flies (*Drosophilia*) are an ideal livefood for surface-feeding fish. A culture can be easily started and maintained using old banana skins in jam jars which are covered with muslin. When provided with a sugar mixture, and kept warm, these flies breed freely, and can be tipped out on to the water's surface. The wingless mutant form is preferable as fish food, because it cannot fly.

Mealworms are another livefood which can be offered to larger fish such as cichlids, and have a high protein content. Their hard outer covering of chitin is a deterrent to some fish, however, and it is preferable to use moulting soft-skinned individuals, which are white rather than yellowish in colour. Mealworms can be kept in bran, to which a vitamin and mineral powder has been added, along with slices of apple on the surface, and housed in a covered container as suggested previously.

FREEZE-DRIED LIVEFOOD

The technique of freeze-drying has revolutionized the availability of livefoods for the aquarist previously dependent on local supplies, but although the process itself was well-known at the beginning of the nineteenth century, it has been widely used only during recent years. The livefood, such as tubifex, is prepared by freezing, to convert all the water present into ice, and this is then removed by drying without actually heating the product. As a result, it retains its flavour and smell, and thus appeals to the fish. For the aquarist, a freeze-dried product can be stored indefinitely in the home and its nutritional quality will not deteriorate. Tubifex is conveniently packed in small blocks, which float on the surface of the water when first added to the tank, attracting the fish to them.

A drawback of the freeze-drying technique is that any bacteria originally present in the livefood will not have been destroyed. This has been overcome by gamma irradiation of foodstuffs, which are then reconstituted by the addition of vitamins destroyed by the radiation itself. These products are sold in foil packets from more specialist outlets, and have to be kept refrigerated.

OTHER ALTERNATIVES

As a change from livefood, ox heart can be fed to considerable benefit to the fish. Studies undertaken in California using guppies have shown that their lifespan could be increased by up to 50 per cent when feeding ox heart every other day. It is prepared by dicing the meat into small pieces, taking care to remove any fat and remains of blood vessel walls. The resulting chunks should then be placed in a liquidizer and blended to the consistency of porridge. Discreet spoonfuls can then be placed in clean plastic bags in a deep freeze until they are hard, and stored for later use. One or two such balls are removed and thawed at room temperature to provide a single feed for the guppies. The major disadvantage of feeding heart is that it soils the water, and cleanliness of the tank assumes greater significance. The fish void whitish droppings on a diet of heart; this is quite normal.

Other meat products can be fed to fish, typically the larger, more carnivorous species, such as piranhas. Canned dog food is often acceptable, but it is important that pieces are cut up very small so the fish cannot choke on them. In addition, if the tin is already opened and thus stored in a refrigerator, the meat must not be fed directly, but allowed to warm up at room temperature first. Dried dog food can also be used, provided that it is well soaked before being offered to the fish.

VEGETABLE INTAKE

Many fish take a proportion of vegetable matter as part of their diet, if given the opportunity. Certain aquatic plants, such as Java Moss are particularly attractive to fish, and they will eat the tops off the growing shoots. Algae in the tank are another source of food, often favoured by mollies, loaches and *Sydontis* catfish amongst others. In a newly-established tank, however, there will be no algal growth, and as an alternative, boiled lettuce or spinach should be provided. Duckweed (*Lemna* species), which floats on the water surface, can be included in tanks for cichlids, which eat vegetable matter, since they will often feed on this plant. Boiled oatmeal, which contains a significant amount of protein, is another alternative food.

FEEDING BEHAVIOUR

You should check regularly that the fish are all eating, because loss of appetite is often a sign of impending illness. Some fish, such as angelfish and discus, can lose their appetite for no apparent reason, however, and may need to be tempted by a change of diet. Any fish which persist in spitting out food should be removed from the tank, as they are likely to have an intestinal complaint.

In the communal tank, feeding time is when bullying is more likely to occur, and slower, shyer fish must be allowed an opportunity to feed unmolested. There is no need to worry over the feeding ability of Blind Cave Characins (*Astyanax jordani*) even in a tank alongside other fish, as they are often amongst the first to find food. They have developed an acute sense of smell to compensate for their lack of vision and only when offered daphnia are they possibly at a disadvantage.

ALGAE AND THEIR CONTROL

Although the presence of algae in a tank can be of benefit to the fish by providing a readily-available source of food, they may also spoil the appearance of the tank if their growth is not kept in check. There are over eighteen thousand different species of alga known, some of which live in suspension in the water, causing it to be cloudy, while others prefer to colonize rockwork and the sides of the tank. These minute plants also occur in a range of colours, from brown and green to blue. Those found in aquaria are often introduced with livefoods, plants or even the fish themselves.

The major predisposing factor to excessive growth of green algae in a tank is too much illumination, and aquaria which are exposed to sunlight as well as artificial light often suffer severely from an explosion of the algal population. A maximum of eight hours total artificial lighting per day is sufficient when no sunlight falls on the tank, and this should be reduced accordingly if the aquarium is in an environment which is naturally well lit.

In the face of a severe rise in algal contamination, the fish themselves may start showing signs of ill-thrift. As with plants, algae utilize oxygen from the water at night, and in sufficient numbers may deplete the supply so that the fish become starved of this vital gas. In addition, algae may poison fish directly by liberating toxins, which accumulate in the water.

When attempting to clean a tank of excessive algae, it may be necessary to transfer the fish elsewhere, and clean the tank thoroughly. Hot water alone, with a temperature in excess of 80°C (176°F), will kill algae, so all parts of the tank, including the gravel, should be left to stand in water for a quarter of an hour or so. This treatment should then be repeated, because algal spores are quite resistant to destruction. The tank itself should be filled cautiously with hot water, and then wiped round and rinsed. It is well worth doing the job thoroughly once, rather than having to repeat it, and this will also be much less disturbing for the fish. The aquarium should then be set up again as before, but in a different location if necessary, or with the amount of illumination reduced. Overfeeding of plants may also contribute to excessive algal growth.

Regular cleaning of the tank on a limited basis is all that is generally needed to keep algal growth in check, rather than complete emptying. The sides of the tank can be easily cleaned from the outside using a magnetic scraper. The cleaning pad complete with magnet is introduced at the top of the tank above water level, and is held in place by another magnet on the outside of the tank. The sides of the aquarium can then be cleaned by moving the magnet outside the tank up and down the glass, which draws the scraper with it, and causes the minimum disturbance to the fish in the process. It is also possible to acquire cleaning pads on long handles which perform a similar function. Special care is needed when cleaning the sides of plastic tanks since these scratch very easily, and their appearance suffers as a result.

Algae will also colonize filters and connecting tubing, which can be cleaned with the appropriate set of brushes. It bears repetition here that the brushes should never be washed out in disinfectant or detergent, because residues are likely to be introduced to the tank when they are next used, with potentially fatal consequences.

Particularly stubborn deposits of algae can be removed directly by means of a clean razor blade (although not recommended for plastic tanks) or a paper tissue. Rubber gloves should always be worn if there is any risk of contaminating the aquarium water with chemicals present on the hands. Brown algae, which is suggestive of inadequate lighting, comes off as distinct scrapings which will then need to by syphoned out of the tank, whereas green algae is softer and adheres well to paper tissues. Various

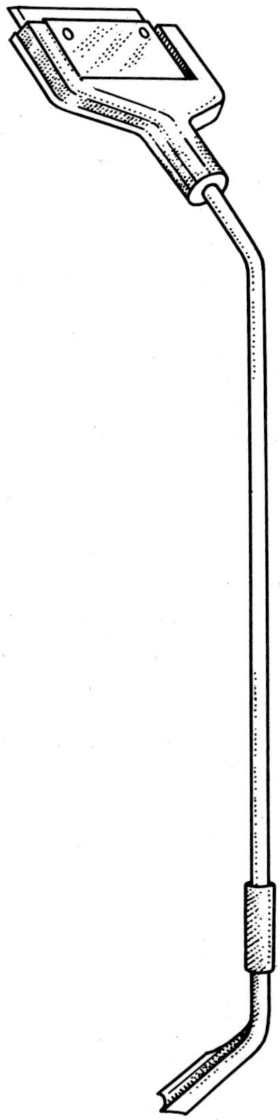

Scraper for removing algae.

aquarium cleaners are marketed to suck out such debris, but a suitable length of flexible rubber tubing, such as that used for bunsen burners, is quite adequate.

Fill the tubing with aged water from a plant watering can, and then cover both ends with a finger. Put one end of the tube in the tank, and the other end into a bucket placed on the floor below the level of the tank; then uncover the end that is in the tank. When you finally remove the finger over the other end of the tube, water will flow into the bucket. This is also a good method of partially changing the water in the aquarium, which should be done every month or so.

Up to one-third of the water in the tank is replaced with fresh 'aged' water. The water you remove from the tank can be used subsequently to good effect for household plants, because of its relatively high nitrate content.

The nitrate level in the aquarium can be monitored by means of a test kit. There is increasing evidence to show that nitrate, formerly thought to be of little significance to the fishes' health, can in fact have a deleterious effect if the level in the aquarium is not kept in check. Plants will utilize some of the nitrate produced by bacterial breakdown of toxic ammonia, but a partial water change is the most satisfactory means of controlling the concentration present in the aquarium. Most freshwater fish can tolerate nitrate levels up to 100 ppm (parts per million), but certain species, such as discus and *Apistogramma* cichlids, are more sensitive, and the level in such cases should not be allowed to rise above 50 ppm.

MAINTAINING AQUARIUM EQUIPMENT

Once the tank is established, its components must be checked closely each day. If there is no alarm system, the thermometer should be watched for any signs of fluctuation in water temperature, which may indicate a defect in the heating system. Damage can, in fact, be caused by the fish themselves, as certain larger species, such as Oscars, may attack heaters or thermostats for no apparent reason. If this does occur, it is safer to protect the heating apparatus behind rockwork, or else by wrapping plastic garden netting around it, fixing the ends with plastic ties. When there is any reason to suspect a fault, the power supply must be disconnected immediately, before anything else is done. Water in its impure state is an efficient conductor of electricity.

The pump will need to be serviced every three months or so, to remove accumulated debris which has been drawn in with the air. Tobacco smoke can be a particular problem, and may be introduced via the pump into the tank with disastrous consequences. Guppies can be killed in this way with very small quantities of smoke, and studies have shown that the exposure of females to smoke blown over the top of the tank causes sterility, and deformed fry in the case of pregnant guppies.

Problems with aeration in the tank may not result exclusively from a defective pump. The outlet tubing might have got blocked or accidentally kinked, which will reduce its efficiency, while air-stones, too, can become blocked. Filter media must also be changed at regular intervals, every two or three weeks or so, depending on the aquarium concerned.

CARE OF AQUARIUM PLANTS

If the plants do not appear to be thriving, the amount of illumination which the tank is receiving may need to be increased. Those which feed through their roots, such as cryptocornes and *Echinodorus* may benefit from the occasional provision of a pellet of fertilizer. Some aquarists use a rabbit or guinea-pig dropping buried nearby in the substrate for this purpose. Alternatively a suitable tonic can be prepared using a proprietary plant food mixed thoroughly with clean clay, rolled into a pellet. A relatively common problem with *Echinodorus* and also *Vallisneria*, especially the Giant form, is that the leaves turn white, and then transparent with new growth appearing retarded. Ultimately the plants start to rot away. This disorder is known as chlorosis, and results from a specific lack of iron in their environment.

Amongst other problems, algal contamination of plant leaves can occur, especially in a tank with catfish, which stir up the substrate. Careful wiping of the leaves will remove this unwelcome growth. The plants in an aquarium will need thinning out occasionally, not only to give the fish more swimming room, but also to prevent their growth becoming stunted. Surface plants such as Duckweed may have to be scraped off regularly using a net, if their growth becomes too luxuriant, to allow sufficient light to penetrate through to plants rooted at the bottom of the tank.

INTRODUCING NEW FISH TO AN ESTABLISHED TANK

There will be a time when new fish are to be introduced to the established tank. This must be undertaken cautiously to minimize the risk of introducing disease, and to protect the new arrivals from bullying. A small quarantine tank is essential, where these fish can be acclimatized to new surroundings and a check kept on their appetites and general health for about a fortnight before they are transferred to the main tank. A second tank set-up is also useful in an emergency against a failure in the main heating system, as the necessary component can be transferred immediately, assuming it has been cleaned after previous use.

CATCHING FISH IN A TANK

When fish have to be moved, they are caught with a net, although in the case of very large fish, an anaesthetic can be added to their water to facilitate capture and to lessen the risk of injury. There are various designs of net available, the majority being made from nylon, although muslin is probably a softer option. Square or rectangular nets are suitable for use in the average tank, and these should be about 10 cm (4 in) in depth, depending obviously on the fish which has to be caught. Nets are quite cheap to purchase, and it is advisable to have a separate one for each tank, because disease can be transferred easily by this means.

Fish net.

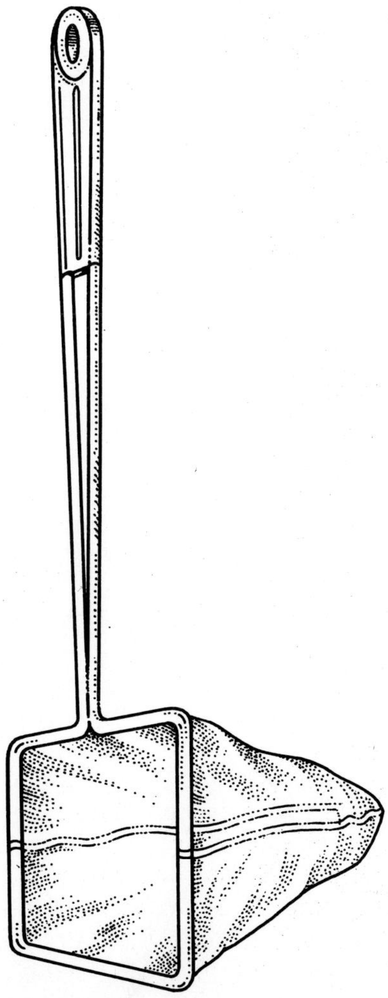

Stealth is needed to catch fish in a tank, as well as patience. Place the net gently in the tank, and move it in the direction of the fish to be caught. It is often easier in a planted tank to catch fish at the front, where there are fewer obstructions, such as rocks or plants, which could snag the net. Once the fish is close to the net, a sudden upward movement of the net should serve to retain it. Use your free hand to cover the mouth of the net once it is out of the water, to prevent the fish jumping out accidentally. Then with minimum delay, transfer the fish to its new environment. Fish should not be handled if possible, and with wet hands if it is essential, to prevent damage to their sensitive skins. Some catfish are dangerous to handle, because of their poisonous spines. The common Coldwater Catfish, a member of the *Ictalurus* genus, is typical of this group and a prick from its spines can prove quite painful.

The rim of a net is relatively hard, and can injure fish, especially those with large fins. Tape bound around the rim will provide some padding, but there is an alternative, safer method for catching such fish. A plastic bag is introduced to the tank and the fish to be caught is driven into the open mouth by a net or planting stick. This technique is probably also less traumatic than direct netting. The bag itself can be 'baited' with daphnia to attract the fish in, if there is no urgency over catching them. Another method, which is very suitable for Spiny Eels (*Macrognathus aculeatus*), as they will disappear into the substrate when threatened, requires a length of rubber tubing of suitable diameter. This is placed on the floor of the tank, and within a few hours, the eels will enter and hide in the tubing, which is then removed with them *in situ*, thus causing minimum disturbance to the remainder of the aquarium.

DEALING WITH A POWER FAILURE

Power cuts present a potentially life-threatening situation for the occupants of a tropical aquarium, and in such conditions it is vital to insulate the tank as much as possible. Thick expanded polystyrene cut to size and fixed around the outside of the tank with adhesive tape is very useful for this purpose, and can even be used on a daily basis to reduce heating costs.

The hood should be left in place, and the top of the tank also covered with a quilt or thick blanket to restrict heat loss. It is safer to disconnect the apparatus from the mains supply, and then plug in again as soon as power is restored. If the lights come on unexpectedly while the hood is covered, there is a danger of a fire starting.

There is no point in disturbing the coverings to check the water temperature, because this will lose vital heat. At room temperature, the water will cool down relatively slowly, enabling the fish to adjust to the change gradually. The reverse process occurs once the heating system is functioning again, and although not recommended, most tropical fish will survive a gradual fluctuation in the temperature of their surroundings. In a dire emergency, paraffin heaters can be used close to the tank; however, as well as the risk of fire, the vapour given off will pollute the water unless the tank is adequately covered.

GOING AWAY

Fish present less of a difficulty at holiday time than other pets, although adequate preparation must be carried out. A partial water change is likely to be beneficial and all equipment should be overhauled. It is also important to check the electrical wiring.

Whilst the average fish can probably fast for two weeks or so without ill effects, it is now possible to obtain both 'week-end' and 'vacation' food blocks. These are placed in the tank and offer a constant release of food to the fish over a given period of time without contaminating the water. If a friend or neighbour who has no experience of fish is persuaded to come in and check the tank daily, it is vital to stress the need not to overfeed the occupants. The provision of a spare heating system, and lighting, will ease the burden on the friendship should any apparatus malfunction during the holiday period.

4 BREEDING

Breeding fish in an aquarium can add greatly to the enjoyment of keeping them. While certain species, like the guppy, can be considered free breeding, there are others which present much more of a challenge for the determined aquarist. Details concerning the breeding requirements of particular fish are discussed under their individual headings, whereas this chapter is concerned with general principles. It is well worth observing and making notes on the breeding behaviour of rarer species, which, when combined with information on the feeding routine and water chemistry, may well add significantly to knowledge about their reproductive habits. Such articles, when published in the specialist fish-keeping magazines, are invariably of benefit to fellow aquarists. There is particular scope for those who wish to concentrate on a specific group of fish to highlight individual differences between the apparent needs of the various species. Serious breeding attempts will, however, necessitate more space for tanks, and increased expenditure on equipment.

CONDITIONING FISH TO BREED

In the wild state, breeding is stimulated by a change in the environmental surroundings of the fish, and this can be mimicked to some extent in aquaria. A varied diet, with an increased level of protein, is recommended for conditioning together with livefood, which encourages activity. If possible, the sexes should be separated for three weeks before being re-introduced. A small increase in the temperature of their water can prove of benefit while longer periods of lighting prove a stimulus for coldwater fish, which are normally exposed to seasonal changes. The condition of the water is significant, and the introduction of a pair to a fresh tank may produce success. With fish which prove reluctant to breed, it has been possible experimentally to inject them with specific hormones to stimulate reproductive activity, but such techniques are not available to the average aquarist.

SIGNS OF BREEDING CONDITION

There are various physical signs which indicate that a fish is entering breeding condition: females appearing fatter, for example. Body coloration often becomes

Male sticklebacks (*Gasterosteus aculeatus*) develop red bellies when in breeding condition.

brighter at this time, and new colours may even appear, as in the case of the male Three-spined Stickleback (*Gasterosteus aculeatus*), which develops a red belly. Most fish when breeding become more active and may turn against other members of a community tank. Fatalities can occur at this stage, unless the fish are separated. If no spare tank is available, you will need to partition the aquarium with a suitable divider.

Cichlasoma salvini, showing breeding coloration.

MODE OF REPRODUCTION

Female fish of some species reproduce by means of eggs, whereas others give birth to live young. In the case of egg-layers, the male fertilizes the eggs once they have been laid, being in close proximity to the female at this time. When live-bearers were first studied in aquaria, it was assumed that males did not copulate with their mates, but released their semen nearby, and that this was drawn into the female's body via the genital opening. Work with platies confirmed, however, that actual physical contact took place, but lasted for only a few seconds. After a single mating, females of the family Poeciliidae can have a number of broods without further contact with a male fish. Paul Hahnel, who helped to establish the popularity of the guppy, recorded the production of seven consecutive broods as the result of a single mating in this species.

Nesting behaviour is not uncommon with fish which are breeding. The Stickleback (*Gasterosteus* species) is a typical example, while various anabantid fish construct so-called 'bubble nests' at the water's surface. These are comprised of air trapped in mucus, giving rise to the bubble, and plants are also often included, serving to anchor the structure in place. Some killifish bury their eggs in the bottom of the shallow pools where they live until the pools dry up. When the next rains come, these eggs, protected in the mud, then hatch, giving rise to the next generation of killifish. As would be expected, these fish reach maturity quickly, by the age of three months, whereas others, such as Blackline Tetras (*Hyphessobricon scholzei*), will not usually breed before six months of age.

Another fish whose eggs survive out of water is *Copeina arnoldii*. In this case, both fish leap out of the water simultaneously, and the female lays her eggs on an overhanging leaf where they are fertilized by the male. Once back in the water, the male remains in the vicinity of the eggs above, soaking them regularly by splashing at the water surface with his tail.

The pairing off of fish is not usually a permanent phenomenon, and a lasting bond is rarely formed. The signs of bonding in the case of Discus (*Symphysodon discus*) are a pair remaining close together, nudging each other and repelling other fish which approach them. Not all fish will accept their intended mates; when Oscars (*Astronotus ocellatus*) are seen snapping at each other's jaws, this is a sign that they will not form a satisfactory pair, and if left together, one may be injured as a result. Indeed, a few cichlids can be rather selective over their choice of mate, and some members of the genus *Channa* may restrict themselves to just one partner.

Members of the cichlid family may not always prove compatible.

A pair of discus. These fish stay in close proximity to each other.

Brood protection in cichlids:
Top substrate spawner (*Cichlasoma meeki*), with young;
Centre young discus fish feeding on the parent's flank;
Above mouthbrooder (*Tilapia*) with young retreating into the parent's mouth.

Mystus catfish may nourish their offspring. *Mystus vittatus* from south-east Asia is shown here.

Any form of parental care for eggs or offspring is rare in the case of fish, although there are exceptions. Some members of the *Tilapia* and *Haplochromis* genera, for example, do not deposit their eggs, but retain them in their mouths until they hatch, and then care for the fry in a similar manner. The female normally carries out this task, but it is not unknown for the male to assist her. When breeding, therefore, these fish do not feed for at least three weeks.

Some adult fish are adapted to nourish their offspring. Young discus nibble for a period on the skins of their parents, while some species of *Mystus* Catfish actually produce a milky secretion which is rich in protein for their offspring. The young fish attach to their parents and obtain nourishment by clinging on by their teeth to a primitive nipple, located on the underside of the adults.

In spite of these isolated instances of parental care, the majority of young fry face a very hazardous existence, and may often fall prey to members of their own species. Eggs are even more vulnerable to predation, so the number produced by egg-laying species is large, usually running into hundreds, and out of these, only a handful of fish will survive to maturity. In species such as the sticklebacks, relatively fewer eggs are laid by the females, but these are protected in a nest rather than scattered randomly in the water. Fish eggs generally tend to sink, and are adhesive by nature, so that they often stick on to plants in the vicinity where they were laid. Vegetation serves to camouflage and protect the eggs until they hatch, which can be a matter of days, or even months later in the case of killifish. Most eggs hatch within a fortnight of being laid, although this will be influenced by the temperature of the water.

In the case of live-bearing species, there is less risk of losses amongst the next generation and consequently fewer fry are produced. This mode of reproduction helps to overcome the critical period when many of the eggs of oviparous species are destroyed. Unlike mammals, however, where the placenta forms a vital link between mother and offspring, there is no such connection in live-bearing fish, and the female's body simply acts as a safe refuge for the eggs until they are ready to hatch. Such species often produce less than 100 fry, which emerge bent in half but soon straighten out. The female carries her brood for a relatively long period, ranging between three weeks and three months in most cases, with the temperature of the water influencing the duration of gestation.

Unfortunately, as with egg-layers, it is not always possible to breed live-bearers successfully in a community tank, because the fry are often eaten. Pregnant females are kept isolated, therefore, to maximize the number of offspring which are reared. If this system is adopted, females should be moved relatively early because they can be upset by rough handling, and their brood is likely to be aborted before the young fish are able to survive independently outside their mother's body.

Bubble-nest builders, such as the Fighting Fish (*Betta splendens*) seen here below their nest, need to be kept in covered aquaria.

The actual set-up of the breeding aquarium is therefore rather dependent on the species concerned, but the tank itself should ideally be 60 × 30 × 30 cm (24 × 12 × 12 in), as this will give adequate space for rearing the potentially large number of fry which may be produced through the early stages, without the necessity of having to move them. The condition of the water in the aquarium must be monitored before the adult fish are introduced. Rainwater can act as a softener, while peat will serve to decrease the pH if required. The state of the water is of particular importance for the successful spawning of certain egg-layers. As a further stimulant, a black water product can be added to the water. This is an extract based on vegetable matter, which aims to mimic the natural environment of the fish in the wild. It can be used for various species, including characins, gouramis and certain cichlids.

The heater in breeding tanks should be positioned vertically, so that fry cannot settle on the glass casing, where they are likely to be injured by the heat. Aeration of the water will help to maintain a constant temperature throughout the aquarium, but it is vital that this is carried out very gently, by means of a fine air-stone. The aquaria of breeding anabantids should not be aerated, however, because of the delicate structure of their bubble-nests, and must always be kept covered.

Haplochromis burtoni – a mouth-brooding cichlid.

Filtration in breeding tanks will help to improve the environment for the fry, and may thus encourage increased growth rates, but can only be carried out safely by an under-gravel filter or a poly-foam sponge type. An additional advantage of the latter is that the fry are likely to find minute particles of food around the sponge. Box and power filters are potentially dangerous for use with fry, since they are likely to suck in and entrap the young fish. Certain box filters are, however, adapted with a fine grid to prevent such losses.

Breeding traps for live-bearers are favoured by some aquarists to protect the brood. While there are various refinements available, the basic trap is a box which fits into the aquarium, with the water temperature equilibrated, and which allows the fry to escape from their potentially rapacious mother. A large trap is preferable, and a small sprig of *Myriophyllum* can be included, to give cover for the female. Breeding nets are another alternative, and the flow of water through these is better than in the case of most breeding traps. In an emergency, breeding nets can also be used to confine a fish in the main tank, if it has been injured.

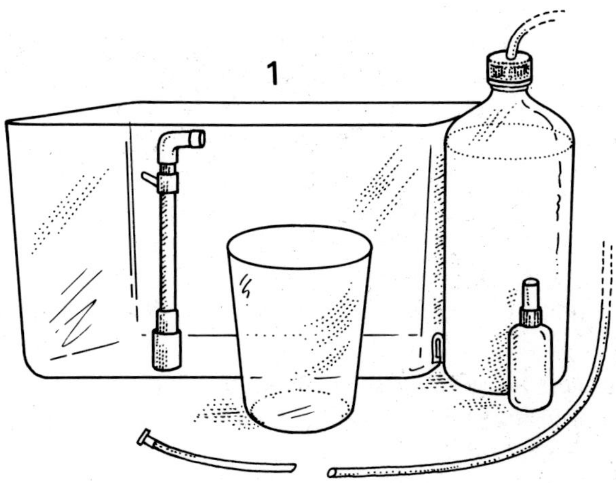

CARE OF THE FRY

The young of egg-laying species tend to be smaller than those of live-bearing fish. There is a considerable discrepancy in their size, however, ranging from cichlids which are quite large on hatching, down to the tiny anabantids. Size alone does not give an indication of the difficulty in rearing them, because some small fry have relatively large mouths and so are easier to cater for successfully. After hatching, the young fish are dependent on the reserves of food present in their yolk sacs until these are exhausted, and during this period they remain inactive, hiding away in vegetation and other suitable sites.

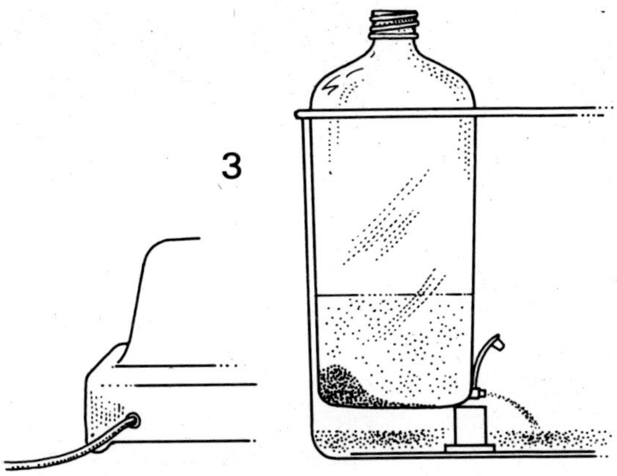

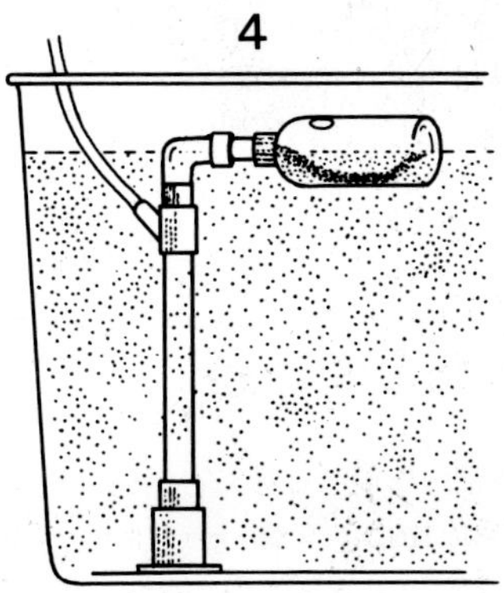

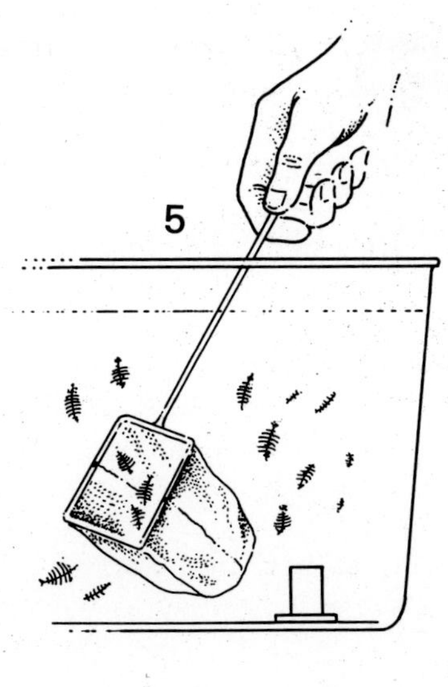

The hatching and rearing of brine shrimps (*Artemia*):
1 the general equipment required;
2 hatching the larvae from the eggs;
3 transferring larvae to the rearing tank;
4 introducing food for the larvae;
5 removing adult brine shrimps for feeding to the fish.

Banded Cichlids (*Hemichromis fasciatus*) are very aggressive towards each other, and cannot be kept in a community tank, but they are very tender in the care of their young.

Young fish need to be kept in a relatively small aquarium, where suitable food is nearby. If they are not in close proximity to food, they are very likely to starve. Since fry are unable to consume large amounts of food, they need to be fed small amounts, perhaps five times during the day.

FOOD FOR FRY

In the case of small-mouthed fry, they will require infusoria or a commercially prepared substitute. Infusoria itself is a collection of minute microscopic organisms which develop in water containing vegetable matter. It is easily prepared by leaving crushed lettuce leaves, banana skins or even turnip slices in a jar of dechlorinated water for several days. Hay can also be used as an alternative, but must first be treated with boiling water, which serves to break down the cell walls. As the culture develops, the water will turn pinkish and cloudy, indicating the development of the protozoa, and then clear. Small volumes can be introduced via a pipette or spoon to the tank containing the fry. Unfortunately the protozoan *Paramecium* will not survive well in heated water, and so must be given in limited quantities. Infusorians are especially useful for newly-hatched anabantids. As a guide, 100 fry will empty a 1 kg (2.2 lb) jam jar of infusoria daily. It is, however, much easier to acquire one of the starter foods, produced for both young live-bearers and egg-layers, rather than to rely on infusoria cultures.

Brine shrimps (*Artemia*) are a very useful rearing food for slightly larger fry, which seek moving livefood. The brine shrimps are purchased from aquatic dealers in the form of eggs, which must be hatched in saltwater. Various methods are recommended for hatching these small crustaceans, and commercial kits are available, but the results obtained are not always successful. The technique outlined here was devised at the University of Ghent in Belgium, and proved itself in the rearing of a large number of young seahorses (*Hippocampus histrix*). It has several advantages over more commonly used methods, although it is slightly more laborious.

The first step is to add the eggs to dechlorinated water, allowing a maximum of 4 g of eggs per 100 cc of water. Allow the water to aerate for about an hour, so that the thick outer covering around the egg is thoroughly permeated by water. Then add an equal volume of 5 per cent sodium hypochlorite and leave the solution to aerate for a further twenty-five minutes. This treatment serves to destroy the hard indigestible shell surrounding the eggs, leaving behind the immature shrimps protected in a membrane. Alternatively it is now possible to purchase decapsulated or shell-less eggs, which makes the hatching process easier and more efficient.

The shrimps, which are then pinkish-orange in colour, must be washed thoroughly under a running tap until no trace of the smell of hypochlorite remains. Finally, transfer them to a suitable container, such as a clean milk bottle containing a solution of 30 g sodium chloride dissolved in a litre of dechlorinated tap water. Given adequate aeration, and kept at a temperature of 25°C (77°F), the napulii, which are the larval form of the brine shrimp, will hatch within about twelve hours or so, which is approximately half the time of more conventional methods. They can then be sieved and offered to the fry.

There is no need to worry about separating the indigestible shells from the nauplii using this technique, because all the shells are removed by chemical means. If inadvertently consumed by the fry, these shells can block their intestines, and also pollute the water unnecessarily. Eggs which fail to hatch are not wasted, as they can be consumed with their shells removed, although not all fry will take them readily.

If you set up several cultures in succession, you will have a constant supply of the shrimps, although it is a false economy to purchase a relatively large quantity of brine shrimp eggs, because they are likely to deteriorate. Once a pack is opened, those which are not being used must be kept in an air-tight container, such as a screw-top jar. The jar itself must be completely dry, because the eggs take up moisture readily, and this seriously affects their hatchability. They must also be kept cool, in a temperature below 29°C (85°F).

In the case of the smallest fry, which cannot cope with brine shrimps on hatching, begin introducing them when the fry are about six days old. Tiny microworms are an alternative source of food. An inert item, which is a reliable stand-by, especially in an emergency, is hard-boiled egg yolk. Separate out fine particles of yolk using the sieves recommended previously for daphnia, or using muslin, so that there is no risk of the fry choking on large particles. Egg yolk must be fed in restricted amounts, however, because any excess will tend to cloud the water.

GENETICS AND MUTATIONS

Mutations in fish arise, as in other animals, when the genes responsible for a particular characteristic, such as colour, are modified. All genes occur on paired structures known as chromosomes, and fish have, in fact, been used as genetic models for the study of chromosomal abnormalities in humans. In the case of the normal male, the pair of chromosomes determining the individual's sex are of differing length, and thus distinguishable from all other pairs. This pair is referred to as XY, Y being the shorter member of the pair.

Dr Hamilton, working at the Downstate Medical School, Brooklyn, New York, selected killifish to further studies into trisomy in humans. He dosed males with high levels of female sex hormones, to turn them into breeding females. From these fish, a proportion of the offspring were YY, mimicking the condition in which a proportion of males have an extra Y chromosome. When introduced alongside normal female and male killifish, these YY individuals proved more aggressive, but lived for a shorter period. The results appeared to correlate with observations on human patients suffering from this genetic abnormality and fuelled speculation that Y chromosomes do have a role to play in determining the individual's lifespan.

Chromosomes are also vital when cross-breeding of species is attempted. Hybridization depends on the individuals concerned possessing the same number of chromosomes. The guppy, for example, possesses forty-six, whereas Siamese Fighting Fish have only forty-two, so it is impossible for these fish to breed together successfully. Hybridization may, however, occur between some members of the community tank. Swordtails (*Xiphophorus helleri*) have been crossed with platies (*X. maculatus*) giving rise to a wide range of attractively-coloured hybrids.

When mutant or hybrid forms first occur, it takes careful husbandry to maintain them successfully. Such stock is often weak with the original strain of golden angelfish, for example, being handicapped by sterility and blindness. The dovetail form of the guppy, first bred in New York, only produced very small numbers in each brood in the early days of its

Breeders have produced numerous colour variants of the Fighting Fish (*Betta splendens*).

Standard forms of Guppy.

bottom sword

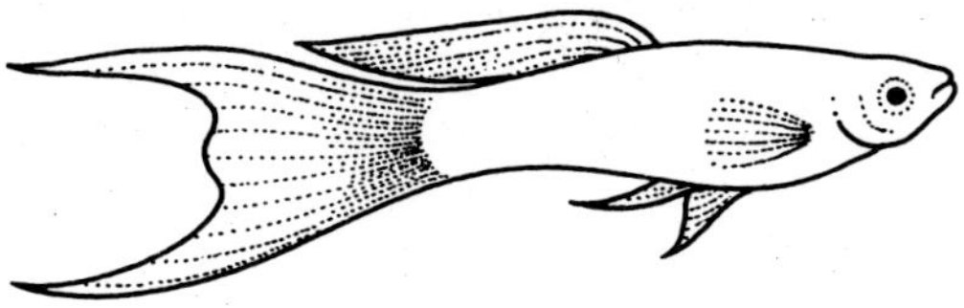

double sword

flagtail

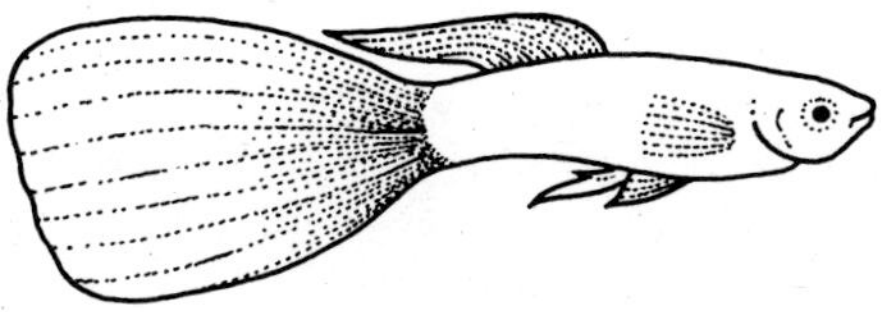

veiltail

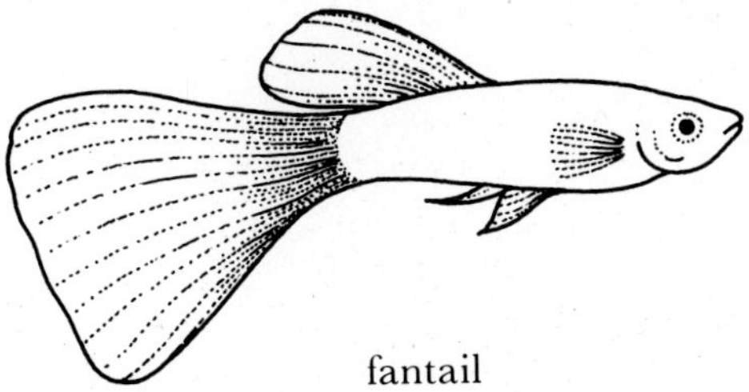

fantail

round tail

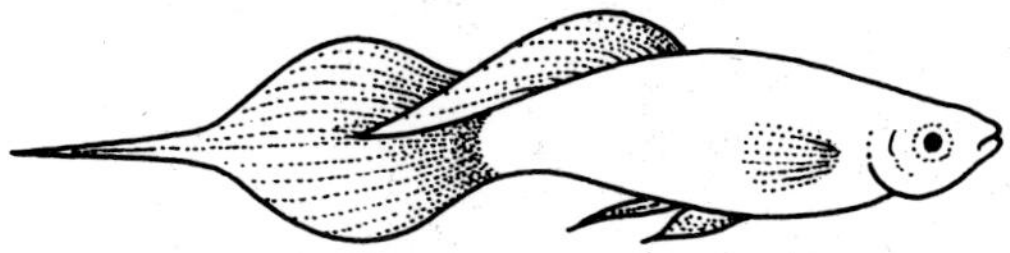

pintail

speartail

spadetail

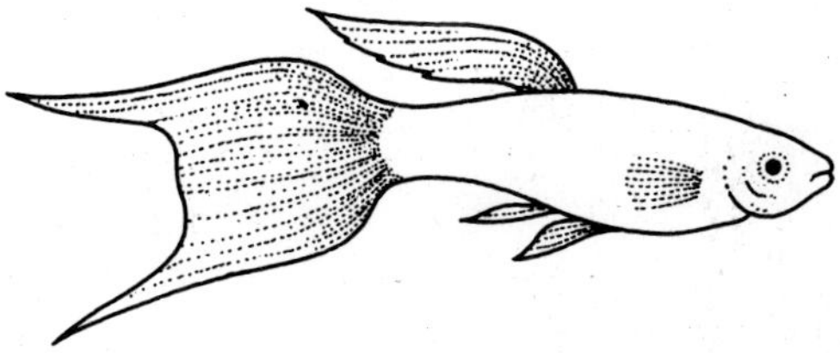

lyretail

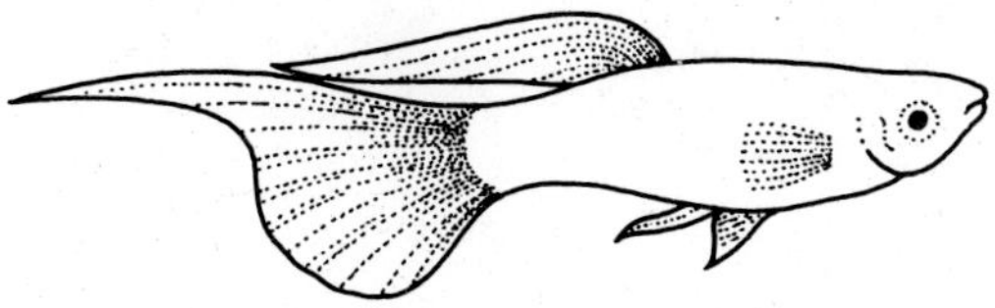

top sword

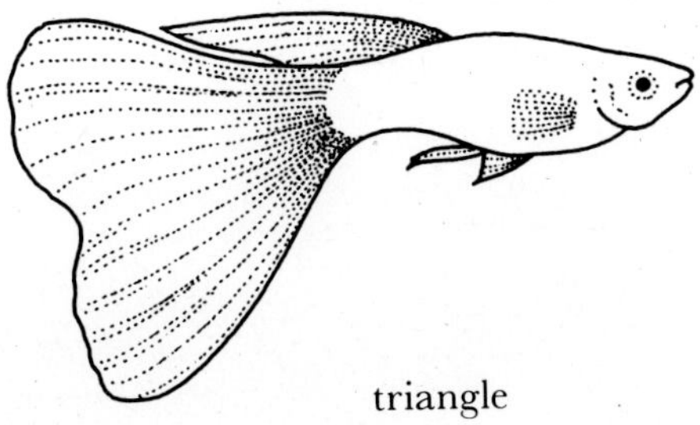

triangle

Hi-fin Swordtail, showing its enlarged dorsal fin.

existence. Indeed, not all mutations are established; some remain elusive. Four albino Fighting Fish were recorded over a thirty-year period up to 1969 in America, but could never be bred in any numbers. Some mutants die out completely, as happened with the so-called Robson Guppy, named after the original breeder, which disappeared shortly after the accidental death of Mr Robson himself. He never revealed the origins of this supposed mutant, and some aquarists felt that it was in fact a hybrid.

Once established, difficulties may persist with a particular mutation. The male Hi-fin Swordtail, which has an enlarged dorsal fin, also often suffers from an abnormally large copulatory organ or gonopodium. This can be cut back, but frequently regrows, and artificial insemination of the females has been used successfully by some breeders to overcome the problem. The technique is facilitated by the use of an anaesthetic added to the water to immobilize the fish. The development of mutations remains controversial in some quarters, and whether such patent deformities as the enlarged gonopodium of the Hi-fin should be encouraged is a question for the individual's conscience.

5 HEALTH PROBLEMS

The majority of diseases that affect aquarium fish can be traced directly back to their environment. The chemical composition of their water has been discussed previously, and significant alterations are likely to have lethal consequences. Sudden changes in pH, for example, will cause convulsions and ultimately death, as essential bodily activities such as heart contractions cease, causing oxygen starvation in other organs, especially the brain. Having set up the aquarium correctly, regular checking of the pH, and partial water changes as suggested previously will eliminate this potential hazard to the fishes' health. Aquarium water naturally tends to increase in alkalinity as a result of the various chemicals which enter solution over a period of time.

DH readings are of particular importance in breeding tanks. If the total hardness is low, then it is not unusual for the fry of some species, such as the Growlight Tetra (*Hemigrammus marginatus*), to succumb with constitutional dropsy before they are even free-swimming. The temperature of the water is another important factor, because as it rises, the amount of oxygen present in solution decreases. Fish suffering from an oxygen deficiency are seen gasping at the surface.

In the well-balanced tank, which is regularly maintained and not overcrowded, such problems are unlikely to be encountered. Strict hygienic precautions over the feeding of fresh livefoods and the introduction of new fish will serve to minimize the risk of disease affecting the tank's occupants. The advances made in feeding fish over the past few years have ensured that nutritional diseases are now rare, although they can still occur. Guppies, for example, are prone to spinal curvature if their diet is deficient in Vitamin C, while fish fed low levels of Vitamin A can suffer from blindness, stunting, and haemorrhage affecting the base of the fins. An excessive intake of fat may result in lipoid liver degeneration, the liver becoming enlarged and covered in haemorrhages, causing the fish to appear anaemic. All possible fat should be removed when preparing offal for fish food.

HELP WITH DIAGNOSIS

When faced with a severe outbreak of disease, the fish concerned can be sent for examination to a laboratory. Contact with such institutions can be made through a local veterinarian, who may also be able to help directly. The current regulations concerning the despatch of diseased fish to a laboratory should be ascertained, and it is often helpful if details such as their housing conditions, diet and symptoms are enclosed. A sample of water from their tank is also often useful to a laboratory. If possible, it is preferable to arrange an appointment and call in person, because it is then possible to take living specimens which are affected, rather than corpses, and these may be of more use to the scientists for their research.

Proprietary remedies are a great help to the aquarist, and should cope adequately with most common problems that can be treated. When using any treatment, however, the accompanying instructions on the pack should be followed closely, because some remedies, especially those containing copper, are very likely to prove toxic if used in excess.

POISONING AND ITS PREVENTION

The possibility of accidental poisoning should always be considered when there are a number of sudden mysterious deaths in a tank. Indeed, many of the chemicals in everyday use around the home, in the form of aerosol sprays, can prove toxic to fish. The air-borne particles will settle on the water surface, if the tank is not covered, and they can be carried on local air currents for a considerable length of time. The threat posed by chlorine, and copper from newly-installed piping, has already been mentioned, as has the danger from cigarette smoke.

BACTERIAL DISEASES

Bacterial infections in fish are generally caused by members of the Gram-negative group, and out of these, the most dangerous is piscine tuberculosis, which was first recognized in 1897 and is still quite prevalent. Losses can be very high during outbreaks of tuberculosis and the symptoms are quite variable, ranging from emaciation to exophthalmia, causing the eyes to protrude unnaturally. Body coloration may fade, while damage to the scales and fins is also often noticeable. Fish affected with tuberculosis are generally lethargic and refuse to feed. Such symptoms can be associated with other diseases, but a confirmatory diagnosis can be made in a laboratory. A veterinarian will advise on carrying out the necessary tests if an outbreak of tuberculosis is suspected in the aquarium.

Although humans cannot contract tuberculosis from affected fish, it is possible for skin complaints to develop following contact with contaminated water or the fish themselves. If the disease is suspected, then rubber gloves should be worn when dealing with the tank. Treatment of fish suffering from tuberculosis is generally not successful, and the aquarium should be emptied and washed out with an iodine-based disinfectant to kill the bacteria. Following a very thorough rinsing, it can then be re-used safely.

DROPSY

This is not a disease in itself, but a description of a symptom. A swollen abdomen is the characteristic sign, but the actual causes may be infectious or non-infectious. *Aeromonas* bacteria can cause dropsy and lead to sudden losses, with fish going off their food. These bacteria are often isolated from cases in conjunction with a virus. Infectious dropsy is seen especially in goldfish, and although treatment rarely proves effective, the complaint itself does not generally assume epidemic proportions.

SKIN DISEASES OF BACTERIAL ORIGIN

Damage to the fins or gills will enable bacteria, as well as other pathogens, such as various fungi, to gain a hold on the unfortunate fish. Some species are more prone to such complaints than others, with fin rot, for example, being commonly encountered in Black Mollies. These can be classed as 'opportunist infections' as no single bacteria is implicated in every case.

In the community tank, fin-nipping can have severe consequences. Certain fish, such as Zebra Danios (*Brachydanio rerio*), are notorious 'nippers' and should not be kept alongside species with long fins, such as angelfish. It is not always easy to spot the culprit, because nipping may occur even when the light is switched off. Close observation will be necessary to spot the aggressor, and suspects may have to be moved to another tank for confirmation.

In order to prevent a bacterial infection developing at the site of a nipped or damaged fin, add neutral acriflavine, or a proprietary remedy used for fin rot, to the water at the appropriate dilution. The water temperature can also be raised slightly to 25°C (77°F). Fins will regenerate quite effectively, although they often remain relatively dark in colour for a long period, until the cell pigments are re-organized.

When dealing with sick or injured fish, it is useful to have a separate hospital tank where they can recover, without having to compete with their companions for food. Treatments added to the main tank may also present problems. Constant exposure to neutral acriflavine over a period of time will decrease growth rate, and can lead to sterility and liver damage. It is said that the use of livefoods, especially daphnia, during the treatment helps to minimize these adverse reactions, but obviously exposing healthy fish to such chemicals is not recommended. If acriflavine is used, it is important that the neutral form, and not the acid preparation, is obtained.

TREATMENTS

Antibiotic treatments for bacterial infections of fish are now being used quite widely, but they are not effective against viruses and only a small proportion have proved useful in counteracting fungal diseases. In Britain, suitable antibiotics can only be obtained from veterinarians, but elsewhere, they are more widely available. It is possible to inject larger fish carefully, but a soluble form of treatment is most commonly used in aquaria. This will usually colour the water, terramycin turning it yellow for example; but more significantly, the antibiotic is likely to destroy many of the beneficial bacteria present in the established tank. The effects can be severe, especially where an under-gravel filter is being used. Fish to be treated should therefore be transferred to another tank.

Other remedies can also damage the bacterial flora. The dye methylene blue falls in this category, and will, in addition, stain the silicone rubber sealant. Some chemicals used to treat fish ailments, such as malachite green, formalin and salt have a less harmful effect if used at the correct dilutions. Unfortunately, many proprietary remedies will be partially inactivated by filtration over carbon, so that in a hospital tank, a basic poly-foam filter is recommended.

PARASITIC DISEASE

Diseases of this group are of particular significance to the aquarist, especially those caused by unicellular organisms known as protozoa. The most widespread disease in this category results from infection by *Ichthyophthirius multifiliis*, abbreviated to 'Ich' or 'Ick', which is the cause of the condition known as white spot. The characteristic small white spots can develop all over the body, but they are only one stage in the life cycle of this parasite.

Actual multiplication of the parasite takes place off the fish. The spots fall off, and the resulting cysts can each give rise to up to 1000 tomites, (the free-swimming stage). They must find a host within about twenty-four hours after hatching, depending on the temperature of the water, if they are not to die. In an aquarium, therefore, the introduction of just one fish suffering from this disease can lead to an epidemic, as the tomites have no difficulty in finding hosts. Overcrowding will make an outbreak of white spot even more serious.

Knife fish with white spot (*Ichthyophthirius*).

The life cycle of *Ichthyophthirius multifiliis* (white spot). When adult, the spherical parasite on the skin of a fish falls to the bottom where it encysts. The contents of the cyst then divide to produce large numbers of motile spores which infect other fishes. At the top is a much-enlarged drawing of the adult parasite showing the typical horseshoe-shaped nucleus.

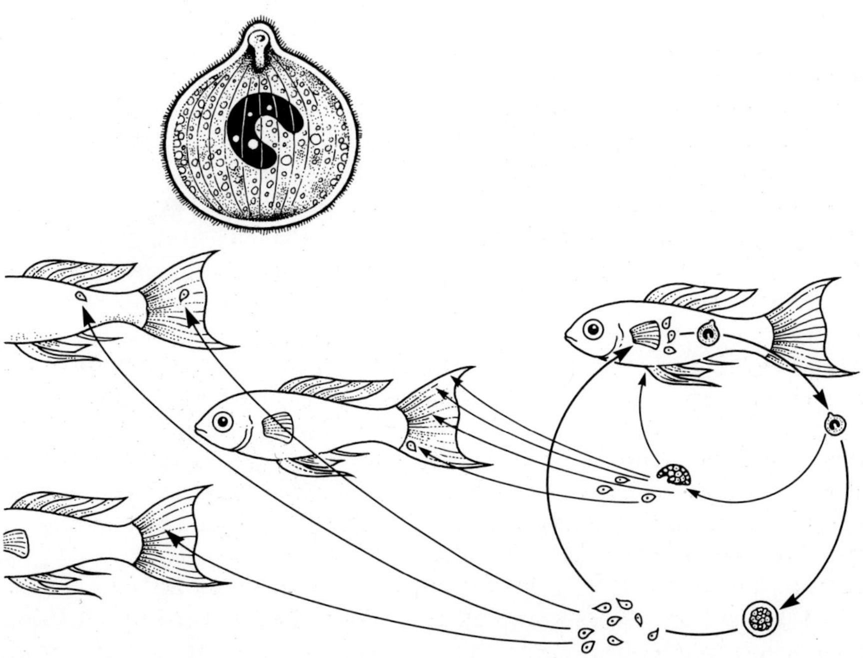

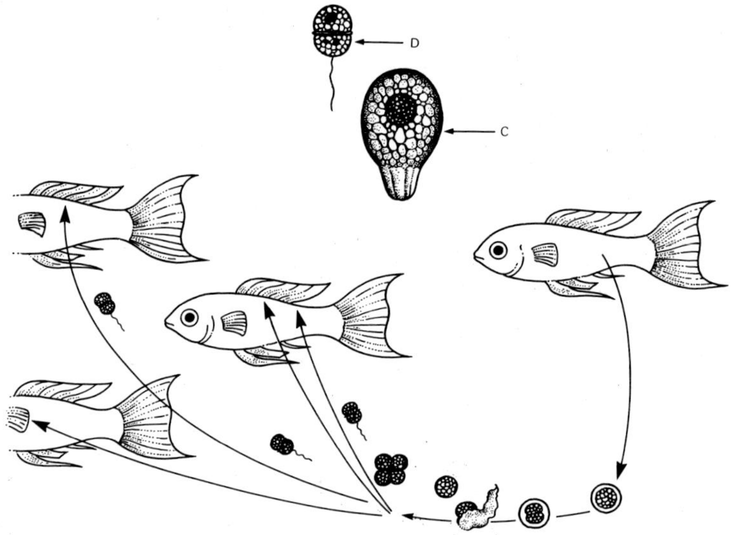

The life cycle of the dinoflagellate protozoan *Oodinium pillularis* is similar to that of *Ichthyophthirius*. The parasites develop on the skin and gills of a fish as tiny white spots, and when mature they fall to the bottom and encyst. Numerous divisions within the cyst (C) produce motile spores, here known as dinospores (D), and these infect other fishes.

The tomites burrow into the fish's skin, giving rise to the characteristic white spot. Here they cause irritation and skin damage, which predisposes to secondary infections by opportunist bacteria and fungi. Once the tomites have embedded to form the trophozoite stage, they are difficult to destroy. Sequential treatment aimed at eliminating all tomites before they can embed, is therefore necessary. Various proprietary remedies are available from aquarist shops, while chemical treatment with formalin, often in conjunction with malachite green, is also effective.

The scale of the disease, and the resulting financial cost, which is estimated at one million dollars per year in America alone, has encouraged research into possible means of preventing it. Early attempts to produce a vaccine were hampered by the difficulties encountered in maintaining the protozoa satisfactorily under laboratory conditions. Working with a closely related species, scientists at the University of Georgia College of Veterinary Medicine achieved a breakthrough, and were granted a patent to produce a vaccine during 1982. Although currently it has to be given by individual injection, it is hoped that the vaccine will be developed for mass administration, either via the feed or in the water. The benefits of this research will undoubtedly become more widely available to all those involved with fish over the course of the next few years.

Apart from 'Ich', there are various other protozoal diseases of concern to aquarists. *Oodinium pillularis* has a similar life-cycle to *Ichthyophthirius*, and like another dinoflagellate protozoa *Amyloodinium* causes Velvet Disease. *Amyloodinium* generally attacks only the gills rather than the whole body. Young fish die readily from Velvet Disease, with labyrinth fish and danios appearing most susceptible. It is not always easy to recognize the disease, but the presence of minute yellowish-brown marks on the body, and the rubbing of the fish itself against rocks to ease the irritation, are suggestive of this complaint.

Amongst other types of parasite, flukes attaching to the skin or gills may be encountered occasionally. Members of the Cyprinidae and Characidae families are most commonly afflicted with such flukes. Those which attack the gills are most serious, and harder to eliminate successfully, since their eggs often prove immune to treatment. Repeated therapy is necessary to destroy the young flukes once they have hatched. They cause irritation to the gill membranes, leading to excessive mucus production which may well prove fatal. Flukes normally gain access to the aquarium either with the fish themselves or with contaminated livefood.

Internal parasites do not usually present severe problems for the aquarist but various worms and trematodes may infect fish. Their life cycles can be quite complex, and involve other creatures, such as snails. Signs of infection are fairly non-specific in most cases, although blindness is often indicative of the presence of trematode larvae damaging the lens of the eye. The fish in this instance is the intermediate host, as the adult form of the parasite is only seen in birds. Exophthalmia (also known as 'pop eye') may be a symptom, but this can also result from other causes, such as tuberculosis. There is no specific treatment recommended for these endoparasites in fish.

FUNGAL DISEASE

Fungal spores can commonly be isolated from fish tanks, but often cause disease only when the fish's skin is damaged in some way. There are many different fungi grouped together in the family Saprolegniaceae, but treatment of all fungal infections is similar irrespective of the specific causal organism. Effective remedies are produced by the major aquatic companies, or malachite green as a 1 per cent solution can be used. Apart from treating affected individuals, it is important to try and identify the precipitating factor. Rough netting or handling may be responsible; if the eyes are affected, this is often a sign that the ammonia levels are too high, and caused the damage initially. Fungal infections show as areas of whitish strands, which can develop to resemble cotton wool in severe cases, and the fish are lethargic. In some cases, fish eggs will also be infected with fungus, and must be treated accordingly. Bumble Bee Gobies (*Brachygobius xanthozona*) are prone to this problem.

VIRAL INFECTIONS

Various viruses affecting fish have been identified, and some of these are particularly significant for the fish farming industry. Spring viraemia of carp is a notifiable disease in this category, seen especially in the spring when water temperatures are rising. It results in haemorrhages around the mouth and gills, and can concern the aquarist because goldfish may also succumb to this virus. The swim-bladder is affected in some cases, typically in younger fish. The rhabdovirus concerned is often identified with *Aeromonas* bacteria, while the various conditions are grouped together as the carp-dropsy complex. There is no treatment for the virus.

MISCELLANEOUS DISEASES

Tumours of various types are not unknown in fish, with goldfish, for example, being susceptible to fibromas. These are usually confined to the head, and show as small, firm lumps. They do not appear to cause the fish much discomfort, but can be removed with surgery. The malignant melanoma is a much more serious skin tumour, encountered in offspring resulting from guppies mated with swordtails. This particular tumour is thought to be of genetic origin.

Constipation is not a serious problem in aquarium fish, but can be seen occasionally. Affected individuals have a trail of droppings attached to their anal opening which they are unable to expel completely. The addition of livefood, such as daphnia, to their diet should cure the condition, and prevent it recurring. Fish fed exclusively on dry diets are most susceptible to constipation.

Bumble Bee Gobies (*Brachygobias xanthozona*). Their eggs are prone to fungal infection.

6 TROPICAL FISH

Freshwater fish can prove quite adaptable with regard to the temperature of their surroundings, as shown by experiments using goldfish. They can spawn in temperatures between 12°C (55°F) and 21°C (70°F), and will adjust over a period of time to live in waters where thermometers register in excess of 38°C (100°F). By way of contrast, tropical species can live in relatively cold surroundings. The temperature of lakes in Kenya may fall as low as 5°C (40°F) for part of the year, and yet the *Tilapia* cichlids will survive adequately under these conditions, and start to breed when the temperature rises again. *Tilapia* cichlids are also living wild in England, occurring in a section of canal fed by hot water from an adjoining glassworks in Merseyside. They were liberated there some years ago, and are now thriving in a water temperature of 21°–26°C (70°–80°F), along with other tropical species such as Convict Cichlids (*Cichlasoma nigrofasciatum*) and various mollies.

The Convict Cichlid has been introduced into a British canal, along with other tropical fish.

Even between aquarists, there may be a slight discrepancy in the temperature at which they maintain a particular species. Continental fish-keepers generally keep fish at slightly lower temperatures than their British counterparts, but the figures given in the following section are an indication of the suitable range. Subsequent maintenance of a relatively constant temperature is of equal significance for the majority of fish.

CLASSIFICATION

Many fish are still referred to by their scientific names alone. This is usually comprised of two words; for example, *Poecilia reticulata* in the case of the guppy. The term '*reticulata*' describes the species, with species being defined as individual populations which can breed together successfully, although under normal conditions such hybridization is unlikely to occur. *Poecilia* is the generic term, shared with other related species such as *Poecilia velifera*, the Sailfin Molly. Similar genera are then grouped together in families, such as Poeciliidae in this case. Classification is sometimes revised as new facts emerge about the fish concerned. Guppies were, in fact, formerly placed in another genus, *Lebista*, before their relationship with other members of the genus *Poecilia* was appreciated.

Poecilia reticulata, male with triangle tail.

FAMILY POECILIIDAE: THE LIVE-BEARING TOOTH CARPS

The live-bearing tooth carps, which include guppies, swordtails and platies, are amongst the most suitable fish for the novice aquarist. The Guppy (*Poecilia reticulata*) is ideal, because it will adapt and breed freely under a variety of conditions. Like other members of the family these fish are easy to sex, the males possessing brightly coloured caudal fins. The female guppy, by contrast, is relatively dull and bigger than her mate. The size of the female is a significant feature when selecting breeding stock,

Below and right, *Poecilia reticulata* – four forms of the Guppy.

because bigger females have proportionately larger broods. This phenomenon was fully investigated by Dr Affleck, who published the following formula based on his studies: Number of fry produced = 5.2L - 15.5 - (0.7L - 14); 'L' in this case corresponds to the female's total length at the time of giving birth. He also devised a special breeding trap to prevent any cannibalism, which would have ruined his results.

Although guppies will live in temperatures as low as 15°C (64°F), they do best when kept in a temperature range of 25°–27°C (77°–81°F), with a near neutral pH and slightly hard water conditions, as for other live-bearers. At a temperature of 25°C (77°F), their gestation period is twenty-eight days. Keeping them at 32°C (92°F) reduces this time down to nineteen days, but also shortens the lives of the females. Guppies can breed successfully in a community tank, but it must be densely planted if the fry are to survive. Adults are not fussy about food, and will eat a variety of prepared and fresh livefoods, as well as vegetation, while their fry can be reared successfully on brine shrimps.

A wide range of fancy mutations are now established, with resulting changes to both the fins and colour of these popular fish. In order to preserve these new forms, pairing of closely-related fish is often necessary, and some of these newer, fancy varieties are more demanding in their requirements than the natural guppy. Colour-feeding can often benefit their appearance, particularly those fish with red markings. Before scientific formulations were available, aquarists used boiled carrots to achieve a good depth of coloration in their fish. The carrots were boiled in a minimum of water, and then chopped very finely and mixed into a paste with Bemax.

Albino Sailfin Molly (*Poecilia velifera*).

Guppies are susceptible to fluke infections, dropsy generally being the first sign. Small swellings then develop on the body, and when these are carefully incised, the yellow immature stage of the fluke *Clinostomum marginatum* will be visible. These must be removed with tweezers, and Friar's Balsam, applied on cotton-wool buds, can be used to dress the wound. Several such treatments may be necessary before the wound heals. Guppies are also prone to body tilt, when they lie at an abnormal angle in the water. This could indicate swim-bladder disorder, but occurs mainly in older fish, and is regarded primarily as a symptom of senility, for which there is no treatment.

MOLLIES

Mollies occur naturally in North America, around the Gulf of Mexico, and are usually found in brackish surroundings. Salt, about a teaspoonful to 4.5 l (1 gal), should therefore be added to their aquarium water. Some species can grow quite large, reaching 15 cm (6 in) in length, and thus require adequate space. Mollies are primarily herbivorous in their feeding habits, and will browse contentedly on the resulting algae if their tank is kept in well-lit surroundings. Boiled lettuce and spinach can be offered as alternatives, or until the algae are established in the tank. Some livefood and dried matter will also be eaten by mollies.

There is one disease to which mollies seem especially prone. It is often referred to as 'Mouth Fungus', but this is incorrect as the infection is caused by a bacterium, typically *Chondrococcus columnaris* or a related species. Treatment using 100 mg of terramycin per 4.5 l (1 gal) of water, can be successful.

One of the most common mollies seen in aquaria is the Black form. This is not, in fact, a particular species, but a hybrid strain developed from black individuals of other species. Another similar form, known as the Lyretail Molly, also has a hybrid ancestry, first being bred in south-east Asia. Mollies require a water temperature between 25° and 28°C (74°–82°F), and with their liking for vegetation, only relatively hardy plants, such as *Vallisneria*, should be included in their tank. Females are larger than males, who can be recognized by the presence of their copulatory organ or gonopodium.

Sailfin Mollies (*P. latipinna*) possess enlarged dorsal fins. Another closely related form is *P. velifera*. These fish must have an adequate swimming area to develop their enlarged tails in aquaria. Various domesticated strains of the wild form are now established, and one of the most attractive is the Black Velifera or Midnight Molly, which has yellowish-orange edging to its dorsal fin. The body coloration of this Sailfin is black, as its name suggests. Mollies normally have about eighty offspring, after a gestation period that can be as long as ten weeks.

SWORDTAILS

The Swordtail (*Xiphophorus helleri*) is so-named after the characteristic caudal fin structure of the male. The lower rays are elongated into a sword-like shape. All members of this genus, which includes the platies, are confined to Mexico and Guatemala in Central America. The wild form of the swordtail is basically green, but selective breeding and hybridization have given rise to a wide range of colours, with red becoming especially prominent.

These fish make most attractive aquarium occupants, especially when kept in groups (or 'schools'),

Above and below: Swordtail (*Xiophophorus helleri*).

Xiphophorus helleri, lyretail form.

and although males sometimes squabble amongst themselves, they will not harm other fish. A tank for swordtails should be heated to between 22°C and 25°C (72°–77°F), and planted around the back and sides, leaving adequate space for swimming in the front. They prefer medium-hard water, and will thrive on a varied diet which includes some livefood.

Breeding does not present any particular problem. As in other members of the family Poeciliidae, when the female is about to deliver her brood, the 'gravid spot' becomes visible near the vent. The spot itself is part of the peritoneum, and once visible, it is not safe to move the female without a serious risk of damaging her brood. If she has been transferred to a breeding trap beforehand, great care should be taken to ensure that it does not become fouled by excess feeding. Live daphnia is probably the best food for fish in such traps; if dried foods are used, they should be given more or less as individual flakes, several times a day to satisfy her appetite.

An alternative is to set up a breeding tank, and then remove the female once she has released her brood. Swordtails may produce over 150 fry at a time, but these will often fall prey to any adults in their vicinity, unless there is adequate cover available in the form of fine-leaved plants. For breeding purposes, only one male is necessary for several females.

The wide range of colours now being bred makes the wild swordtail seem a rather insignificant fish. While some of these are described simply in terms of colour, such as Red or Golden, others are named after places which contributed to their development, such as the London, Wiesbaden and Berlin Swordtails. The 'green' type referred to by some aquarists is really a refined form of the wild swordtail.

PLATIES

Platies are very similar in their requirements to swordtails, and are now included in the same genus, although previously they were classified as *Platypoecilus* species, which gave rise to their common name. Two distinct forms, *Xiphophorus maculatus* and *X. variatus* are recognized, the latter type sometimes being known as the Variegated Platy, although they will hybridize quite readily, and various colours are now firmly established. Hybrids produced between platies and swordtails are also fertile. Among the various platies recognized by aquarist societies are Red, Yellow, Black, Blue, Spangled, Leopard, Wagtail, Moon and Sunset forms. Gnat larvae are a popular livefood with these fish, which can be fed as for swordtails.

Xiphophorus maculatus.

OTHER LIVE-BEARING TOOTH CARPS

There are various other members of the family Poeciliidae which may be seen occasionally, including those belonging to the genus *Gambusia*. These fish are not recommended for the community aquarium though, because they are inveterate fin-nippers and prove rather aggressive. They have, however, proved useful in controlling mosquito larvae in areas where malaria is endemic, as they will consume their body weight of these insects daily. The smallest known live-bearer is *Heterandria formosa*, sometimes referred to as the Mosquito Fish, which reaches barely 2.5 cm (1 in) in length. These fish are often bullied by larger inhabitants of mixed tanks, and may even be eaten in some cases. Females produce several young daily over the course of a fortnight, and can have a brood every four weeks or so.

FAMILY HEMIRHAMPHIDAE: THE HALF-BEAKS

Apart from the live-bearing tooth carps, some other fish also give birth to young directly. These include members of the family Hemirhamphidae, commonly known as Half-beaks, because of the unusual arrangement of their jaws. The lower mandible is elongated and immobile, while the upper one is much shorter. Several species are occasionally available, with

Dermogenys pusillus being most common. These fish occur in south-east Asia, and are found in both fresh and brackish waters, and even out to sea in some cases. Males can be recognized by the presence of red on their dorsal fins, whereas females are larger, being approximately 8.75 cm (3½ in) in length. It is inadvisable to keep more than one male in an average tank, since they will often fight amongst themselves when housed in a group.

Half-beaks live close to the water surface, and a temperature of 23°C (73°F) suits them well. When first acquired, they are often very nervous, and must be treated with caution. Their prominent lower jaw is easily damaged, which can prove fatal, and although regeneration may take place in less severe cases, it is rarely ever complete. A tank for half-beaks should have a good surface area, and contain floating plants for cover. They feed largely on insects captured near the surface; fruit flies are especially valuable for them as a source of food. Gnat larvae, daphnia and tubifex in a feeder are other possible alternatives. Food must be available at the surface, because half-beaks will not scavenge near the bottom of the tank.

When breeding, females should be transferred to a shallow tank containing about 15 cm (6 in) of water. They produce between fifteen and forty fry as a rule, which will take fruit flies and brine shrimps from an early age. The gestation period itself can be as long as two months, and it is not uncommon for the female to abort her young during this time. The young fish prefer a higher temperature than the adults, in the region of 28°C (82°F). Although half-beaks are not recommended for the novice, they present a challenge, and make unusual tank occupants.

Dermogenys siamensis – a species of Half-beak.

7 EGG-LAYING TROPICAL FISH

As a general rule, egg-layers are harder to breed successfully than their live-bearing counterparts, and a separate breeding tank is necessary to ensure satisfactory results. Once the eggs have been fertilized, adults which show no parental care should be returned to the community tank. Failure to do this will result in the loss of a large number of eggs in many cases. Fish are generally transferred a couple of days or so before spawning is expected, and are not always fed over this brief period, in order to keep the water as clean as possible for the fry.

ANABANTIDS (Labyrinth Fish)

Members of the family Anabantidae have a unique anatomical adaptation, referred to as the labyrinth organ, which allows them to breathe air at the water's surface. They live in areas of muddy water with a low oxygen content, and must take in atmospheric oxygen in order to survive. The Paradise Fish (*Macropodus opercularis*), found in eastern parts of Asia, is a typical member of this group. They are often rather too aggressive for the community tank, and should really

Fighting Fish (*Betta splendens*) mating.

be kept on their own. Water which is medium-hard and heated to 24°C (75°F) will meet their needs, while the tank itself should be densely planted, complete with floating vegetation.

Glass jars containing the brightly-coloured Fighting Fish (*Betta splendens*) never fail to attract attention in aquarist shops, and various mutant forms are also available. Males, as their name suggests, will fight ferociously among themselves, and, with their long flowing fins, are best kept out of a community tank. A small aquarium, only 60 cm (24 in) in length, and a temperature slightly higher than for the preceding species, will suit them well. Females are much less conspicuous than males, with smaller fins. At breeding time, the male entwines with his mate and is responsible for transferring the eggs to the bubble nest, characteristic of these and other anabantids. The fry emerge in about two days, and, after consuming their egg sacs, will take infusoria.

The gouramis also belong to this family, and are much more suitable for the community tank, although problems may arise at spawning time. The Kissing Gourami (*Helostoma temmincki*), from south-east Asia, has developed elaborate lips for feeding on algae, and 'kissing' contacts can occasionally be observed between two individuals. *Trichogaster* species such as the Pearl Gourami (*T. leeri*) are also popular aquarium

Helostoma temmincki, green and pink forms.

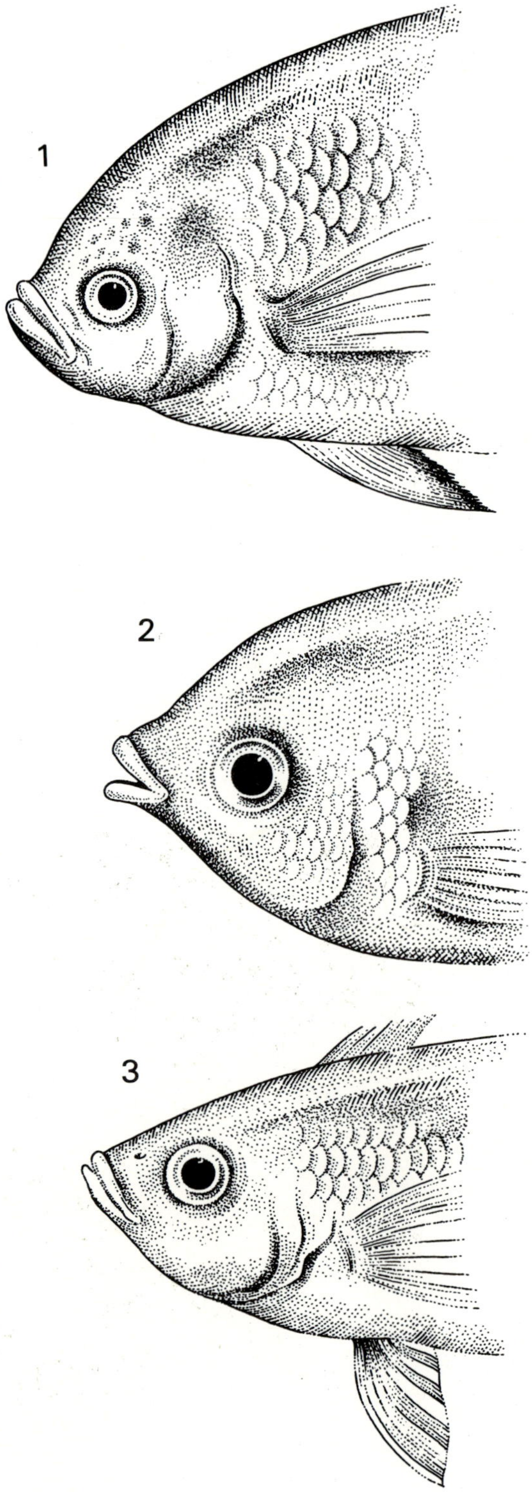

Heads of anabantids:
1 Gourami;
2 Kissing Gourami;
3 Climbing Perch.

Fighting Fish (*Betta splendens*). Three males of different colour forms.

Top, *Trichogaster trichopterus*, selected form known as the Cosby gourami. **Above**, Trichogaster trichopterus, original form.

fish, requiring medium-hard water with a temperature of 26°C (79°F) and a mixed diet. The Chocolate Gourami (*Sphaerichthys osphromenoides*) is an exception from other gouramis, as it must be kept in very soft water, with an acid pH (0–3°DH; pH 6 or less), which is heated to 28°C (82°F). It is not recommended as an introduction to the group, being more delicate than other species. Although African anabantids, belonging to the genus *Ctenopoma* are sometimes available, they are not suitable for the mixed tank, proving aggressive and carnivorous.

Pearl Gouramis will breed in the typical manner of the family, often choosing to build a nest amongst Indian Fern. Males of this species rarely get aggressive towards females after spawning. The eggs hatch in two days, and may yield up to 1000 fry. The spawning tank, as for all labyrinths, must be covered, to prevent excessive losses when the young start

Pearl Gourami (*Trichogaster leeri*).

breathing atmospheric air, which is potentially too cold. Overcrowding will also reduce their numbers dramatically, so the tank should have a large surface area. These can be prolific fish, however, and over eighteen months, it is possible to rear as many as 5000 fry successively from a pair. They require infusoria at first, and fine egg yolk, followed by brine shrimps.

CATFISH

The catfish are a very large group, with over 2000 recognized species divided into twenty families. Many are, however, unsuitable for the community aquarium because they grow too large, and you should bear this in mind when purchasing a particular species. Catfish possess characteristic sensory barbels close to their mouths, which may have a feathery or unbranched structure. Many are semi-nocturnal, preferring to scavenge for food during hours of darkness.

The armoured *Corydoras* catfish are a favourite group for the aquarium, partly because of their relatively small size. They rarely exceed 10 cm (4 in), and are quite active during daylight. These catfish are suitable for a community tank, where they will consume food left by other inhabitants. Several should be kept together if possible, under soft-water conditions with a neutral pH reading. *Corydoras* catfish will breed in the aquarium. Females become swollen with eggs prior to spawning, and should be placed with several males in a lightly planted tank lined with sand, in a temperature of 26°C (79°F). Once a pair is formed, the other males should be removed, and after spawning, these fish must be returned to the community tank because they will eat their eggs. These are laid in batches, numbering a maximum of about 300 eggs in total. They should hatch in about a week, and the fry must be offered infusoria at first.

The Bronze Corydoras (*C. aeneus*) is one of the easiest species to breed successfully. Their tank should contain adequate hiding places, as with all catfish. Spawning occurs from about October onwards, being stimulated by livefoods such as tubifex. They will gulp air directly from the surface, which is a natural adaptation for survival in poorly-oxygenated waters. The two smallest members of the genus are less commonly seen. The Pygmy Catfish (*C. hastatus*) reaches a size of about 4 cm ($1\frac{1}{2}$ in), whereas *C. cochui* is approximately 1.25 cm ($\frac{1}{2}$ in) shorter.

Bronze Corydoras (*Corydoras aeneus*).

Upside-down Catfish (*Synodontis nigriventris*).

Amongst other catfish, those belonging to the family Mochocidae are essentially nocturnal. The unusual Upside-down Catfish (*Synodontis nigriventris*) belongs to this group. It swims upside-down, and thus can feed on the under-surface of leaves. Its pattern of camouflage is also reversed. Two other colourful members of this African genus are *S. angelicus* and *S. flavitaeniatus*, although these tend to lose their markings as they get older.

Synodontis angelicus (above), with *Synodontis flavitaeniatus (below)*. The markings of these fish tend to fade as they grow older.

CHARACINS AND RELATED FISH

Members of this family Characidae have a wide distribution through Africa and tropical America. They are characterized predominantly by the presence of teeth and the development of an adipose fin. Over 100 species have been kept successfully in aquaria, and the family includes some of the most colourful freshwater species. They are not difficult fish to cater for, requiring a water temperature between 21° and 24°C (70°–75°F). Although some are mainly vegetarian in their feeding habits, and others carnivorous, they will live well together if given a mixed diet supplemented with livefood. Unfortunately, they are not frequently bred in aquaria, but some successes have been achieved by providing soft water heated to 28°C (82°F), with plenty of vegetation in the tank where females can scatter their adhesive eggs. These will be eaten, however, if the adult fish are not removed after laying has occurred.

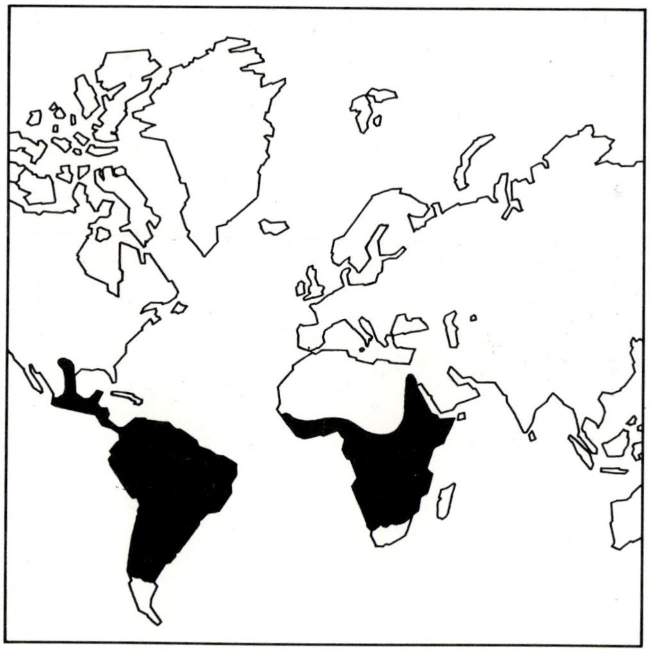

Distribution of the characins.

Piranhas
The most notorious characins are undoubtedly the piranhas, of which four species are recognized. These fish occur naturally in shoals, but in aquarium surroundings, smaller individuals may be cannibalized by their fellows and they are best kept singly.

Piranha (*Pygocentrus piraya*). This species can grow to 60 cm (2 ft) in length.

Cardinal Tetras (*Cheirodon axelrodi*).

Piranhas are, in fact, relatively sluggish fish, and apart from their supposed novelty value, do not make very attractive tank occupants. They require soft, slightly acid water and restricted lighting. Young piranhas can be fed on tubifex and whiteworm, while larger fish will consume ox heart and earthworms. The keeping of piranhas is banned in certain areas, such as the state of Florida, because of fears over deliberate irresponsible releases of these fish and the resulting potential damage to native fish stocks, as has been seen in Australia.

Tetras

The colourful tetras are a particular favourite of many aquarists. The Neon (*Paracheirodon innesi*; formerly *Hyphessobrycon innesi*) and Cardinal (*Cheirodon axelrodi*) are among the most commonly available species. When the Neon Tetra was first introduced to aquarists in 1936, however, it commanded a price of 40 US dollars, which was equivalent in real terms to an average month's salary at that time. Coming from the headwaters of the Amazon, these fish should be kept in schools along with other peaceable fish of similar size, such as small rasboras, barbs or even other tetras. They require relatively dark surroundings, and clean, well-aerated soft water, with a pH tending towards an acid reading (6.0–6.5). This is a carnivorous species, and should be fed accordingly, using prepared foods as well as livefood. They often prefer to eat food which is slowly sinking in the tank. Neon Tetras are regarded as being slightly delicate by some aquarists, especially when young. They are susceptible to Neon Tetra disease, which results in a loss of pigmentation, and is caused by a *Microspordium* parasite, called *Plistophora hyphessobryconis*.

Spawning tanks from these tetras must have dark bottoms, and be kept shaded, as their eggs are sensitive to excessive light. Egg-laying may take three hours or so, during which time perhaps 150 eggs will have been attached to the spawning mops. The parents must then be removed. The eggs should hatch in about a day, with the fry swimming freely four days later. The youngsters should be kept in the same tank water if possible for the first two months of life, because they can react badly to being moved to fresh water. The Black form of the Neon Tetra (*Hyphessobrycon herbertaxelrodi*) occurs in parts of Brazil, and has similar needs. Other tetras of this genus include the Blood Characin (*H. callistus*) and the Bleeding Heart Tetra (*H. ornatus*). Neither is easy to sex.

An unusual species is the Blind Cave Characin (*Astyanax jordani*) which is found in the subterranean caves of the Rio Panuco in Mexico. They are not difficult to maintain in aquaria, and an artificial cave structure can be easily constructed using rockwork and slate. The sensory lateral line is well-developed in these fish. Another tetra with a slightly bizarre

Neon Tetras (*Paracheirodon innesi*).

Blood Characin (*Hyphessobrycon callistus*).

Above, Bleeding Heart Tetra (*Hyphessobrycon ornatus*).

Below, Congo Tetra (*Micralestes interruptus*).

Above, *Ephippicharax orbicularis*.

Below, *Moenkhausia sanctaefilomenae*.

X-ray Fish (*Pristella riddlei*).

Marbled Hatchetfish (*Carnegiella strigata*).

appearance is the X-ray Fish (*Pristella riddlei*) which is semi-transparent. Males in this case are more colourful than females. They can lay up to 300 eggs during a single spawning, but these will be eaten unless the adults are separated from them.

Tetras belonging to the genus *Moenkhausia* are similar to previous species in their requirements, requiring water with a DH of about 10°, and an acid pH which can be achieved by filtering through peat. They have more conspicuous scales than other tetras, and, being omnivorous, may nibble at plants growing in their tank. *Ephippicharax orbicularis* needs a similar tank set-up, with an area for swimming at the front and some tough plants like *Echinodorus* around the perimeter. Floating vegetation on the surface provides both shade and a ready source of food.

African characins, by way of contrast, are less streamlined than their American relatives, but require similar conditions, with adequate space for swimming. They range in size from the Long-finned Characin (*Alestes longipinnis*) which can reach 14 cm (5½ in), down to the Congo Tetra (*Micralestes interruptus*) which is only about 7.5 cm (3 in) in length.

Hatchetfish

Members of this group are not always easy fish to maintain successfully, and are rarely bred in aquaria. Hatchetfish, with their unusual shape, live near the water's surface, and are reported to be able to fly above it as well, using their pectoral fins. They must be kept in a covered tank, and fed livefoods such as fruitflies sprinkled on the surface. Hatchetfish are not really suitable for the newcomer to the hobby of fish-keeping.

Headstanders

These are unusual fish, which often prove difficult to acclimatize to new surroundings successfully. Headstanders remain vertical in the water for long periods, concealing themselves amongst suitable vegetation. They are best kept in shoals in fairly large, well-planted tanks which should always be covered. Headstanders are adept at grazing on algae, and will also consume various worms and other livefood.

Pencilfish

These fish are placed in the family Hemiodontidae, only possessing teeth in the upper jaw, although they are otherwise rather similar to characins, in spite of their slender, elongated shape. They require a well-planted tank with adequate cover where they will often stay relatively motionless unless threatened. Soft water conditions, with a temperature of 24°–26°C (75°–79°F) and livefood will keep them in good health. The Three-banded Pencilfish (*Nannostomus trifasciatus*) and related members of this genus are unique because their markings alter between day and night time. They are rarely bred, and invariably prove bad egg-eaters if given an opportunity to display this vice.

Striped Anostomus (*Anostomus anostomus*) – one of the most attractive of the headstanders.

Three-banded Pencilfish (*Nannostomus trifasciatus*).

The habitat of *Anostomus* and *Poecilobrycon* on the Rio Cucuçamba, north of Obidos in the central Amazon region.

CICHLIDS

Members of the family Cichlidae have a very wide distribution, and while some, such as the angelfish, are well-known to aquarists, others occurring in the Rift Valley Lakes are often rarities which command high prices. Cichlids, with some exceptions, are not good inmates for the community tank, and should really form part of a more specialized collection. They tend to be bullies, and are often destructive.

The two species of Asian Cichlid are quite scarce, although the Orange Chromide (*Etroplus maculatus*) may be seen occasionally. This species is not aggressive or destructive, but is rather sensitive to water changes. Amongst the South American forms, one of the most desirable is the Blue Acara (*Aequidens pulcher*) which is omnivorous and relatively peaceful, only growing to a length of 15 cm (6 in). Eggs are usually laid on suitable rockwork rather than vegetation, and both parents then look after the young fry.

Dwarf cichlids require a similar water temperature, about 24°C (75°F), and a maximum hardness of 10°DH along with an acid pH. These fish are more delicate than their larger relatives, and must have adequate shelter in their tanks, as well as swimming space. Males are generally bigger and more colourful. Spawn is deposited in a prepared cavity, and in the case of *Apistogramma ramirezi*, both adults care for

Distribution of cichlids.

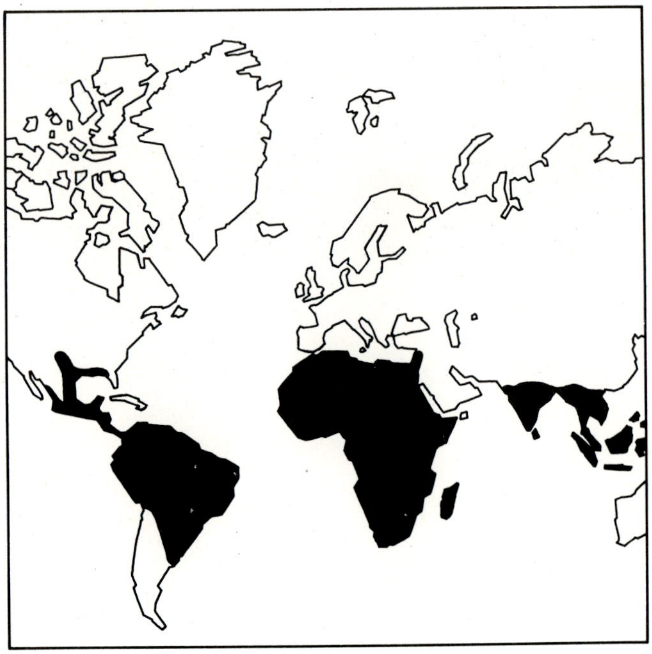

Haplochromis moorii. A mouth-brooding cichlid found in Lake Malawi. Both sexes develop the prominent forehead in this species.

their offspring. The eggs hatch in about four days and brine shrimps can be used as a rearing food along with chopped whiteworm.

One of the most spectacular cichlids is undoubtedly the Oscar, also known as the Velvet Cichlid (*Astronotus ocellatus*), which can attain a length of nearly 35 cm (14 in). Even if small when acquired these fish will ultimately need a large tank to themselves. They are not easily bred, and lay on rockwork which they clean beforehand. The brood may number as many as 1000 fry, which are concentrated protectively in an area by their parents, but only about 300 are likely to survive under good conditions. Fry will consume each other, and they have large appetites. A red form of the Oscar is now being bred in increasing numbers.

There are various other similar but aggressive South American cichlids often available. These include the Jack Dempsey (*Cichlasoma octofasciatum*) named after the famous boxer, and the smaller Zebra or Convict Cichlid (*C. nigrofasciatum*) which grows to nearly 10 cm (4 in). A water temperature of 21°C (72°F) suits these fish well. Both have a tendency to dig into the aquarium substrate, and will uproot plants in the process.

Ramirez's Dwarf Cichlid (*Apistogramma ramirezi*).

Oscar (*Astronotus ocellatus*).

Red form of the Oscar (*Astronotus ocellatus*).

Angelfish are amongst the most popular aquarium fish, possessing a very elegant shape and motion. Youngsters are often sold for community tanks, but angelfish are best kept alone in individual shoals for several reasons. They have a fast rate of growth, and will often outpace other members of the tank, while their elaborate fins invite nipping. Angelfish are predominantly carnivorous in their feeding habits, and will readily consume the eggs and fry of other fish sharing their accommodation. By virtue of their shape, and the fact that they can grow to 15 cm (6 in), these cichlids require a fairly deep tank, planted with suitable vegetation such as *Vallisneria gigantea.*

Their water should be at a temperature of 24°C (75°F) raised a couple of degrees for spawning purposes. A slightly acid pH, about 6.8, is preferable. They will often spawn on slate, and guard the eggs and resulting fry. Various mutations of the angelfish

Pterophyllum scalare, normal form.

Pterophyllum scalare, a selected mottled form.

The three species of *Pterophyllum* can be distinguished by the shape of the head:
1 *P. dumerilii*;
2 *P. scalare*;
3 *P. altum*.

1

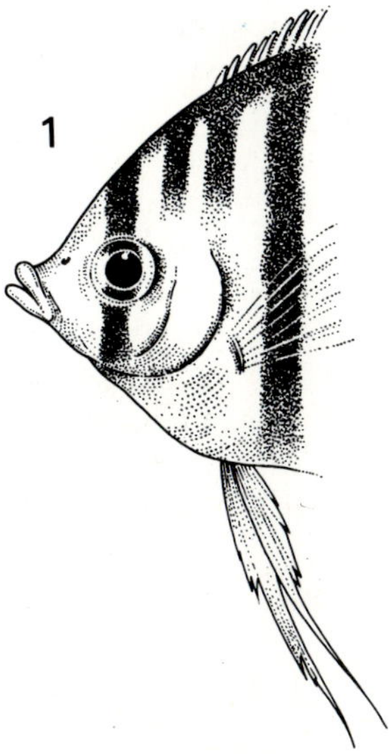

2

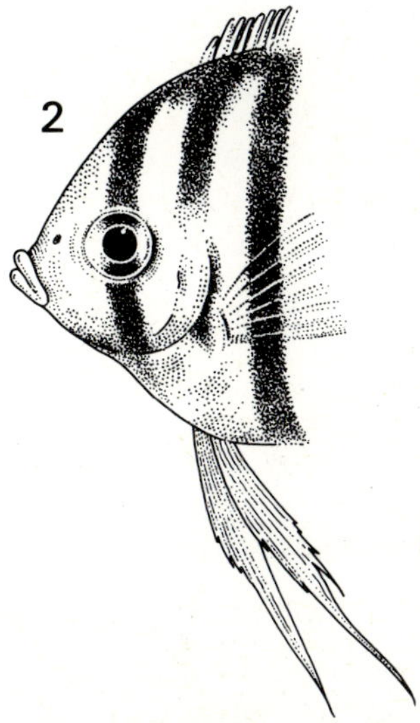

3

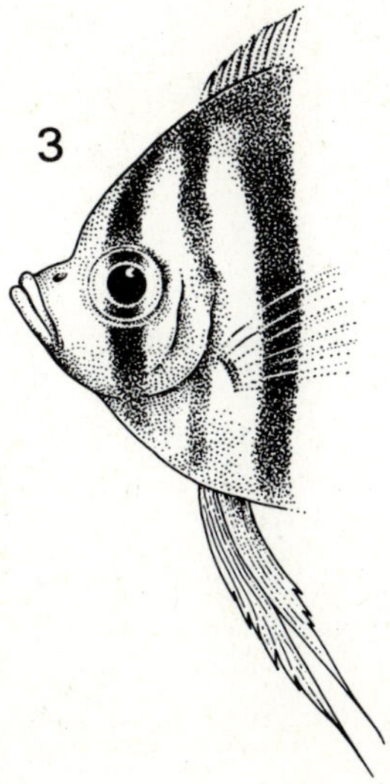

Method of feeding in *Pterophyllum*:
1 the food is seen;
2 the mouth is protruded;
3 the food is sucked in;
4 the mouth returns to its original position.

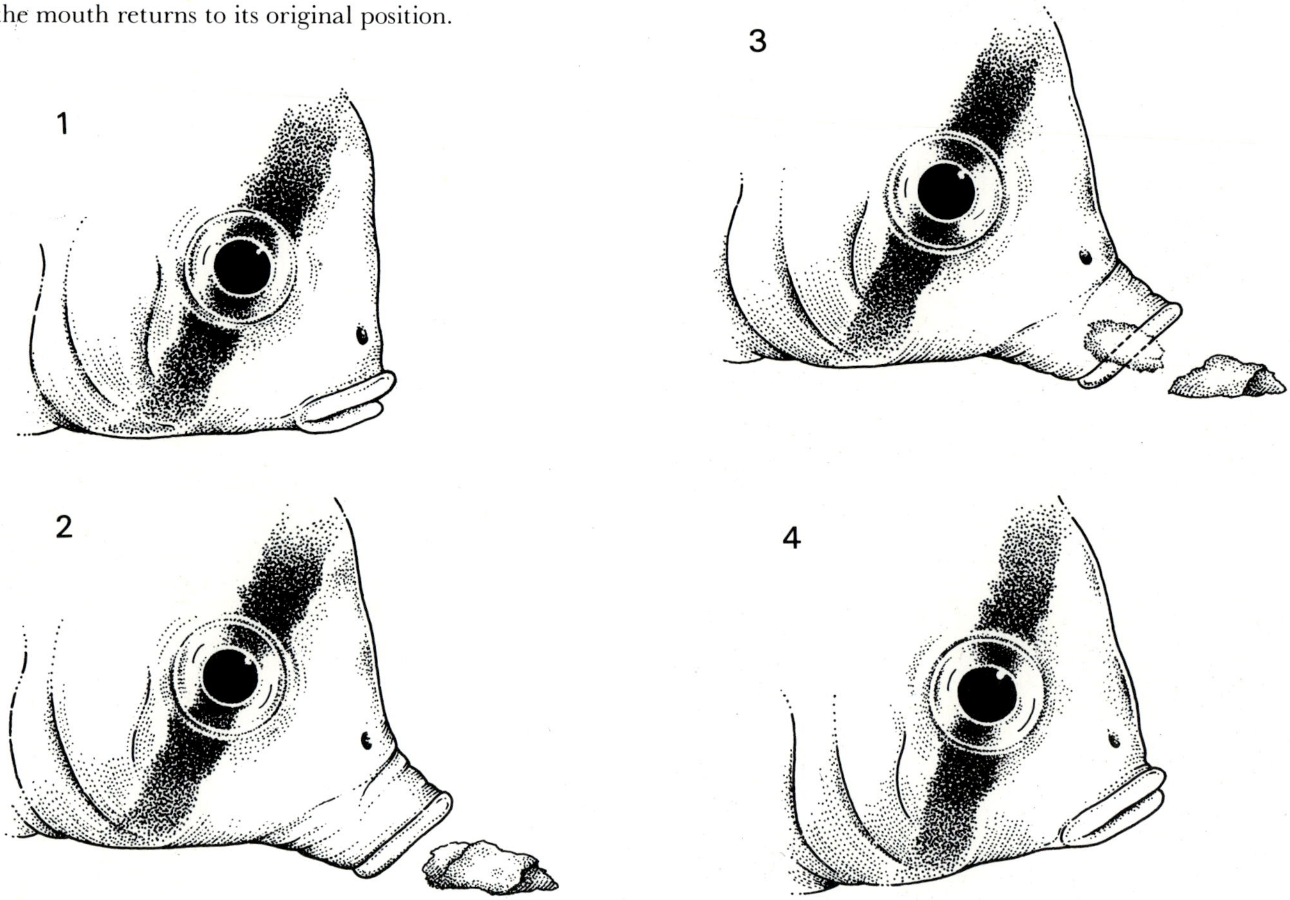

are now established, with such exotic names as 'Butterballs'. These fish become bright yellow as they mature, and were developed initially over a four-year period by Carl Naja in America.

Another very attractive South American cichlid, which requires rather special management, is the Discus, of which two species are recognized. *Symphysodon* require very soft water, with a DH reading in the range 1°–5°, and an acid pH of 6.2–6.6. They are very susceptible to infection by the protozoan *Hexamita* and to various gill-flukes, and cannot be recommended for the novice aquarist. Several attractive colour variants of the Discus have been bred successfully, including a turquoise form produced by Jack Wattley in Florida.

Typical habitat of the discus (*Symphysodon discus*) at Igarapé Curubau, near the entry of the Rio Branco into the Rio Negro.

The turquoise discus, a selected form.

The turquoise discus produced by Jack Wattley of Florida.

Discus (*Symphysodon aequifasciata*). This species occurs from the mouth of the Amazon to Peru.

Turquoise form of the Discus.

Apart from the specialist African Rift Lake Cichlids, other species occur in lakes and rivers elsewhere on the continent. Members of the genus *Tilapia* have even been introduced successfully to other countries, ranging across south-east Asia to Hawaii. These fish are known as mouth-brooders, and some, such as the Mozambique species (*T. mossambica*), can grow quite large, over 30 cm (12 in) in this case.

CYPRINIDS

There are approximately 1500 members in the family Cyprinidae, many of which are popular aquarium occupants. Although the goldfish is best-known out of the group, species in the genera *Barbus*, *Danio* and *Rasbora* are often represented in tropical tanks. The family as a whole is characterized predominantly by the absence of an adipose fin, and the development of barbels in many cases. These have a sensory function, helping the fish to locate food around the substrate of their environment.

Distribution of the carp and barb family (*Cyprinidae*).

Barbs

The tropical barbs are confined to south-east Asia and Africa, with no representatives of the genus present in America. They usually occur in shoals, and should be kept in groups in aquaria. Barbs are not difficult to maintain, requiring a water temperature in the region of 24°–25°C (75°–77°F) and relatively hard water conditions. Cryptocornes are ideal for planting in a tank to house barbs. These fish will accept a varied diet, although their lively natures are most apparent when they are offered livefood. Water in the tank must be well aerated, because in the wild most barbs occur in flowing rather than still water.

Members of the genus *Barbus* can be bred under aquarium conditions, and are not costly to purchase in the first instance. A large number are regularly available, and out of these, the Rosy Barb (*B. conchonius*) is one of the most attractive, the breeding male assuming a bright red colour, offset with a black spot on each side of the body towards the tail. The scales, which are a prominent feature of many barbs, are especially noticeable in this species. These fish require clean, clear water conditions, being found naturally in areas of running water in the eastern regions of India.

Rosy Barb (*Barbus conchonius*).

Breeding condition can be stimulated by increasing the amount of livefood in their diet. Rosy Barbs are one of the easier species to breed successfully. They require a tank furnished with plenty of vegetation in thick clumps, and two males to one female can give better results. They will eat the eggs readily after spawning, and so must be removed as soon as possible. A covering of glass marbles over the floor of the tank will help to protect the eggs, which can then slip down between the marbles. The fry require infusoria or a commercial substitute on hatching, and later can be introduced to brine shrimps.

Typical barb habitat in south-east Asia.

The two species of Tiger Barb (*B. tetrazona* and *B. pentazona*) are also quite prolific breeders. The two forms can be distinguished by the number of vertical stripes across their bodies. They are similar to Rosy Barbs in their requirements, but cannot be trusted in a community tank with long-finned fish, because they are bad 'nippers'. Individuals often prove worse in this respect than a school, possibly because they lack the distinct pecking order which evolves therein. The Five-banded form (*B. pentazona*) is the more reliable community member.

One of the smaller species, rarely exceeding 6 cm (2.5 in), is the Black Ruby Barb, which is a native of Sri Lanka. They prefer a slightly higher temperature than other barbs, about 26°C (79°F) suiting them well. Males develop a rich red tinge to the lower part of their bodies when in breeding condition. In contrast, the Tinfoil Barb (*B. schwanenfeldi*) may attain a length of 30 cm (12 in) or more. It is a striking fish, with a bright metallic silver body and reddish markings on its fins. They require a correspondingly large set-up, taking into account their size, and are

Barbus conchonius.

Barbus nigrofasciatus.

Tiger Barb (*Barbus tetrazona*).

best kept in groups. Tinfoil Barbs have healthy appetites, and bigger specimens will take meat in the form of ox heart and dog food, which must be soaked thoroughly beforehand if necessary. The water in their aquarium needs to be kept clean and well aerated. They are rather susceptible to the presence of chlorine or excessive amounts of carbon dioxide dissolved in the water.

An unusual African barb is *B. callensis*, known also as the Moroccan Barb. This inhabits hot water springs, and is reputed to be able to survive in very high temperatures. Apart from Morocco, it occurs in parts of Algeria and Spain. As it requires an average temperature of 30°C (86°F), this barb will probably need a tank to itself. The attractive yellowish Congo Barb (*B. callipterus*) is not as free-breeding as its Asian relatives. Further south, the Banded Barb (*B. fasciolatus*) occurs in Angola and likewise is rarely seen in aquaria. This species is bluish-green in colour.

Danios

Two members of the genus *Danio* are well-known to aquarists. The Bengal Danio (*D. devario*) from India reaches a size of about 10 cm (4 in) and is silvery-green in colour. It is less often seen than the Giant Danio (*D. sequipinnatus*), found naturally in western parts of India as well as Sri Lanka. The predominant colour in this fish is steely-blue, with yellowish bands running along the body. Females are usually bigger than males, reaching 15 cm (6 in), and their central blue stripe is said to curl more near the tail. This species should be kept in schools with fish of similar size, because they may occasionally eat smaller individuals.

Danios will adapt to quite a wide temperature range, between 21° and 27°C (70°–80°F), and are undemanding with regard to pH and hardness of the water, providing it is not extreme in either case. They take flaked foods readily, and livefood is a very useful conditioner. When breeding, danios should be housed in a tank containing fine-leaved vegetation. A temperature of 26°–27°C (78°–80°F) will induce spawning, and the female should be allowed to settle in the tank for a day before two males are introduced. The adults must all then be removed before they can eat the eggs, which should hatch in a day. The female may well be ready to breed again about a month later.

Other danios belonging to the genus *Brachydanio* are often kept. The Pearl or Gold Danio (*B. albolineatus*) is a fairly ready breeder, which typically spawns in the morning, being stimulated by the sunlight. This species may produce over 200 eggs, but the fish will rapidly consume them if they are given the opportunity. Zebra Danios (*B. rerio*), so-named because of the striped pattern of their markings, are amongst the easiest species to spawn successfully. They can be kept safely in schools with other small fish. Females can be recognized by their rounded bellies. A slightly smaller species, about 3.75 cm (1½ in) in length, is the Spotted Danio (*B. nigrofasciatus*). This fish is often more reluctant to breed than the previous danios, although the fry are not hard to rear on infusoria and then brine shrimps.

Zebra Danios (*Brachydanio rerio*).

Spotted Danios (*Brachydanio nigrofasciatus*).

Brachydanio albolineatus.

Rasboras
Rasboras are confined to south-east Asia, where approximately thirty species are found. They are shoaling fish, and out of the dozen species which are often available, although they adapt well to aquarium conditions, breeding successes are rare. This may be because they are communal breeders, or a reflection on the composition of their water. It is known that they require acid water, with a relatively high concentration of iron, and naturally spawn in masses of cryptocornes and other similar broad-leaved plants. Their eggs are laid on the under-surface of the leaves.

Red Rasbora (*Rasbora heteromorpha*).

Rasboras nevertheless make attractive aquarium occupants, and can be quite long-lived. They require a temperature similar to danios, and are peaceful in a community tank. Sexing is difficult in most species, although there are exceptions, as in the case of the Brilliant Rasbora (*Rasbora einthoveni*), the male of which has a purple tinge. The Harlequin Fish or Red Rasbora (*R. heteromorpha*) is one of the most attractive members of the group, and like Hengal's Rasbora (*R. hengeli*) it requires soft, acid water (pH 5.6–6.4; DH less than 8°). When kept outside such conditions, it is said to become sterile. Both these species reach less than 5 cm (2 in) in length.

Scissortail Rasboras (*R. trilineata*) are characterized by their distinctive tails. Like other related species, they are omnivorous, but prefer livefoods. The Scissortail is a relatively hardy rasbora, and does not require such shaded conditions, with floating plants, as the preceding species. It can grow to 15 cm (6 in), but rarely attains this size under aquarium conditions. The Yellow Rasbora (*R. elegans*), which is rather greyer than its name suggests, is another larger species. It can grow to 13 cm (5 in), and mature females lack the brown tinge seen in the anal fins of males.

For those attempting to breed rasboras, gnat larvae are a good conditioner. The female will spawn in a water temperature of 27°C (80°F) on suitable plants, and is often stimulated by rays of sunlight. In some cases, such as the Red Rasbora, although the eggs are often unmolested, the fry, which hatch about a day later, may well be eaten by the adults. Once free-swimming, the young fish will require infusoria or a suitable substitute. The Eye-spot Rasbora (*R. dorsiocellata*), named after the black spot on its dorsal fin, is one of the easiest species to breed successfully.

Some other cyprinids
The Flying Fox (*Epalzeorhynchus kalopterus*) and its relative (*E. siamensis*), which was only discovered during the 1950s, are useful members of a community tank. They require relatively soft water and a temperature of 23°–27°C (74°–80°F) and being found naturally in fast-flowing water, are correspondingly active. *E. siamensis* is a larger species, with a more yellowish body.

The mouths of these fish are adapted to graze on algae, and also serve to anchor them in a particular locality against a strong current. They live around the bottom of a tank, where they should be provided with suitable hiding places. Apart from consuming algae, Flying Foxes will also eat any *Planaria* which inadvertently are allowed access to the tank, as well as boiled spinach and various proprietary foods. There appears to be no information concerning their breeding habits.

Another cyprinid fish, in spite of its misleading name, which feeds on algae is the Red-tailed Shark (*Labeo bicolor*). It does best in a well-planted aquarium, with soft, acid water maintained at a temperature of 24°–26°C (75°–79°F). Natives of Thailand, these fish tend to become rather quarrelsome amongst themselves as they get bigger. They are very agile swimmers, and can be difficult to catch as a result. The bright red coloration of their tails may be improved by

Above, Scissortail Rasbora (*Rasbora trilineata*).

Below, Red-tailed Shark (*Labeo bicolor*).

Red-fin Shark (*Labeo frenatus*).

Flying Fox (*Epalzeorhynchus kalopterus*).

Apocheilus lineatus, with the male above.

colour feeding, and although omnivorous, Red-tailed Black Sharks must have some vegetable matter, such as algae, cooked oatmeal or boiled spinach available.

Breeding details of this species do not appear to have been recorded, but the closely related Red-fin Shark (*L. frenatus*) has been spawned successfully in an aquarium. They appear to mature at about 7.5 cm (3 in) in length and are often very aggressive at spawning time. Males alone typically care for the eggs until they hatch, which in a temperature of 24°C (75°F) will take about two days. The fry, which may emerge without yolk sacs, can be reared on infusoria and then brine shrimps and spinach. The adults in one case were left safely with the fry after hatching, taking them to shelter if there appeared to be any risk of danger. By the age of seven weeks, there were about 150 fry from this spawning and these had grown to about 1.87 cm ($\frac{3}{4}$ in) in length. A duller member of this genus sometimes available is the Harlequin Shark (*L. variegatus*), which hails from Upper Zaire in Africa. Its requirements are similar to those of the preceding species.

Distribution of toothcarps.

KILLIFISH (EGG-LAYING TOOTH CARPS)

Killifish are perhaps more suitable for the specialist aquarist, and are best kept in individual groups comprised of one species only. Over 500 different types are recognized, some of which have a seasonal life cycle, living in ponds which dry up for part of the year. They require soft water conditions, and some aquarists collect clean rain water for their tanks. In certain areas, however, because of industrial pollution, rain water contains dissolved nitric and sulphuric acid, and so its pH value may be too low. Although some killifish prefer acid conditions, others should be kept in neutral water.

These fish have a very wide distribution, and their breeding requirements are quite variable. Eggs may be laid on plants, while other species burrow in the substrate to prepare a suitable site. The fry may take weeks, months or even years in some cases to hatch, often being naturally stimulated by rainfall. It is possible to buy eggs and hatch them, rather than purchasing fish directly.

Members of the genus *Aplocheilus*, such as the Blue Panchax (*A. panchax*), live at the surface of the water, and should be kept in a tank with floating plants like *Ricca*. These killifish require livefoods such as tubifex and fruit flies to form the major part of their diet, although they also accept some dried food. Amongst the most colourful species are those classified in the genus *Aphyosemion*, which occur in parts of Africa. The Lyretail (*A. australe*) is frequently seen, and requires a water temperature of about 22°C (72°F), with soft, acid conditions. *Epiplatys* species lay on plants, and can be considered for a mixed tank. Males are bigger and more colourful than females.

The *Nothobranchius* killifish occur in eastern coastal regions of Africa, and reach a maximum size of about 6.25 cm (2 ½ in). They are bottom-spawners and will lay on a peat medium which should be provided as the substrate for their tanks. Fruit flies and other livefood like daphnia will prove acceptable to these fish. The easiest species to maintain are *N. orthonotus* and *N. palmqvisti*, requiring a temperature between 22° and 24°C (72°–75°F), and water which is both

Orange-red Lyretail (*A. a. hjerresenii*) – male.

Aphyosemion gardneri.

Lyretail (*Aphyosemion australe australe*), with female in the centre.

Epiplatys longiventralis. A West African species, growing to about 6 cm (2¼ in).

Blue Panchax (*Apocheilus panchax*).

Nothobranchius rachovii.

acid (pH 6.8) and soft (6°–10°DH). *N. rachovii* is slightly more delicate, needing softer and more acid water (2°–5°DH; pH 6.5).

Amongst the American killifish, those belonging to the genus *Cyprinodon* occur in the desert areas of the United States, in the south-west of the country. They need hard, brackish water (15°–25°DH), and a temperature of 25°–27°C (77°–81°F). These species, and those of the South American *Pterolebias* genus lay in the substrate of their tanks, which should be aquarium peat, about 3.75 cm (1½ in) in depth. Male *Pterolebias* can become very aggressive when breeding. Softer water conditions (with a DH of less than 10°), and a lower temperature of 22°C (72°F), with an acid pH, will suit these killifish well.

Cyprinodon macularius, male below.

Typical habitat of *Cyprinodon macularius*, at Saratoga Springs in the USA.

MORMYRIDS

A playful species with an unusual appearance is the Elephant-nosed Fish (*Gnathonemus petersi*), a member of the Mormyrid family. The mouth in these fish has evolved to form a proboscis. They need a temperature

Head of a mormyrid.

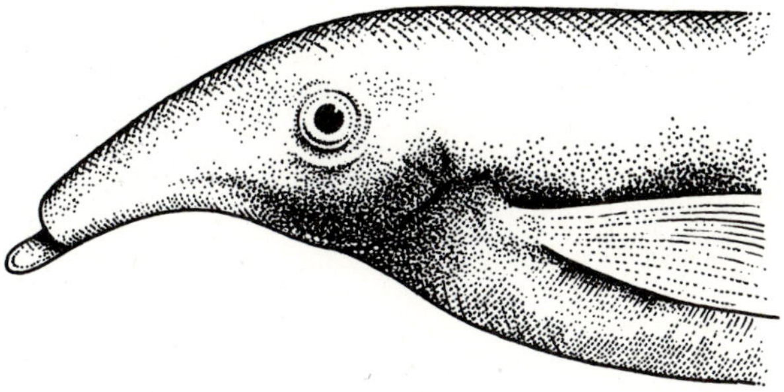

of about 24°C (75°F) and adequate hiding areas in the tank, as can be provided by roots and rocks. Dim lighting suits them best, and the water should be soft. They need plenty of livefood and may grow to a maximum size of nearly 20 cm (8 in). If two young specimens are kept together, they will often play with a small ball made of tinfoil floating on the water in their aquarium. Larger groups should not be housed in the same tank, because they produce electrical currents which can disorientate others nearby. This characteristic serves as an additional sensory device, and in conjunction with it, mormyrids have evolved a correspondingly large brain. They do not appear to have been bred successfully in aquaria as yet, and older individuals may quarrel between themselves.

Elephant-nosed Fish (*Gnathonemus petersi*).

Spiny Eel (*Mastacembelus armatus*).

SPINY EELS AND LOACHES

Spiny eels, like many catfish, are essentially nocturnal. They often occur in brackish water and so salt should be added to their aquarium water, as suggested for mollies. *Macrognathus aculeatus* can reach a size of 35 cm ($13\frac{1}{4}$ in) whereas another Asian form, *Mastacembelus armatus* may grow as large as 80 cm (31 in). Spiny eels feed largely on worms of various types, and should be kept in a tank with a sandy bottom, into which they will burrow, leaving only their heads exposed. They tend to be aggressive, and are rather specialized in their needs.

Acanthopthalmus loaches may at first sight appear similar to spiny eels, by virtue of their long thin bodies. They require similar conditions, and are also more active under conditions of subdued lighting. The various species of this genus are known as Coolie Loaches, and reach a size of about 8 cm (3 in). They have a painful spike in front of their eyes to catch the unwary, and will take air directly from the water's surface. These loaches need soft water, with a DH not

Clown Loach (*Botia macracantha*).

Tiger Loach (*Botia hymenophysa*).

Mouse Botia (*Botia horae*).

in excess of 10°, and a temperature between 24° and 28°C (72°–82°F). They will take a varied diet, and scavenge effectively in the tank. Breeding under artificial conditions is uncommon.

Various other loaches are sometimes available, including the rather aggressive Tiger Loach (*Botia hymenophysa*). The colourful Mouse Botia (*B. horae*) is, by way of contrast, fairly peaceful and requires a temperature of not more than 26°C (79°F). Clown Loaches (*B. macracantha*) are equally attractive, and need soft water conditions.

Another useful loach for the community tank is *Gyrinocheilus aymonieri*, which will consume algae. These fish like well-oxygenated, clean water and a temperature in the range of 20°–28°C (68°–82°F). They have a sucker mouth, and can adhere to rockwork or even the sides of a tank. Since they are then unable to take in water, they have evolved an extra orifice to enable water to continue flowing over each set of gills. Sucker loaches should not be kept alongside elongated fish; they may attach themselves to them, and damage the skins of their hosts.

Loach of *Acanthophthalmus* sp.

Gyrinocheilus aymonieri.

8 COLDWATER FISH

As their name suggests, this group of fish do not require the water temperatures demanded by tropical species. They can be kept in an unheated aquarium, with suitable hardy plants such as *Elodea*, although in some cases the water temperature may need to be raised to encourage spawning. A hood for the aquarium is recommended, so that lighting can be provided and evaporative loss kept to a minimum. Some of these coldwater fish can be transferred to an outdoor pond for the duration of the summer. In such cases, care should be taken to ensure that there is no discrepancy between the water temperatures of the aquarium and pond.

GOLDFISH

Goldfish are undoubtedly the most popular coldwater fish and, having been domesticated for centuries, are now bred in a wide range of colours and shapes, some forms being considered grotesque by all but their most loyal supporters. A Chinese scientist, Shisan Chen, has estimated that no less than 126 distinct breeds of fancy goldfish have resulted from the original form. While the true goldfish can reach a size of 30 cm (1 ft) or more, the fancy varieties are generally smaller.

Goldfish can be obtained in a range of colours, from black and reddish-golden to yellow and silver, with speckled forms also available. Young goldfish are dark green at first, bordering on black, before lightening to their characteristic golden hue. Fry kept in dark surroundings from birth are slower to obtain their colour than those living in well-lit aquaria. The fish's colour can also be altered by changes in the tissue under its scales. Where the cells are modified, their ability to reflect light is altered as a result. These are referred to as 'calico' or 'nacreous' fish. In cases where the reflective layer is absent, the fish is described as being 'matt'.

The Shubunkin is a nacreous variety that otherwise resembles the normal goldfish, although its tail is more ornamental, and the lobes of the fins are slightly rounded. Its name is derived from the Japanese term meaning Vermillion Variegated Goldfish, which describes the mottled appearance of these fish. All nacreous fish must be variegated, those showing shades of kingfisher blue being considered most valuable. Two forms of the Shubunkin are recognized, the Bristol being distinguished from the London form by virtue of its larger fins, and more streamlined proportions.

Another hardy, basic variety is the Comet, characterized by its enlarged, pointed tail and fins. The Sarasso Comet, which is often available, is red and white in colour. Comets are active fish, and need spacious surroundings if they are to show to good effect. They are bred in both normal and nacreous forms, although the latter variety are no longer exhibited. There is a considerable interest in breeding goldfish for show purposes, and standards are established for many varieties. Other fish are also exhibited, and details of enthusiast clubs are listed in the appendix. Alternatively, contact with exhibition breeders can usually be made by studying the advertisement columns of the fish-keeping periodicals, which are also listed. Buying from a breeder is the best means of obtaining quality exhibition goldfish, as such stock will have been selected with regard to the show points of the fish.

Fantail goldfish, as their name suggests, have an elaborate divided tail, as well as additional anal fins. Their bodies are less streamlined than the normal goldfish, being rounder in shape. Both scale types are recognized. Veiltails bred from Fantails have an even more elaborate caudal fin, causing it to hang in folds. They appear very graceful in an aquarium, but care should be taken to ensure that there are no rough edges on rocks, for example, where they could damage their trailing tails.

A variety, resembling the two previous forms in the

Veiltail goldfish, different varieties.

Veiltail goldfish.

arrangement of its tail fins, but instantly distinguishable because of its jet black colour, is the Moor. There is no calico form in this case. It is not easy to maintain the black appearance of Moors, however, because older fish of this type turn bronze rather than remaining black in colour.

Moors also have protuberant eyes, and are thus referred to as being 'telescope-eyed'. The eyes are usually positioned as for normal fish, but occasionally may point forwards. Various types of telescope eye are recognized by the enthusiast, and described accordingly, such as the 'segmented sphere' form. Protuberant eyes are not, in fact, evident in the fry, but usually develop when they are several months old. Fish with such eyes are virtually blind, but can detect their food without difficulty by means of scent.

One of the most unattractive goldfish mutants has been ascribed the exotic name of 'Lionhead', although the German description of 'Tomatohead' is perhaps more fitting. The heads of these fish are enlarged, and have an appearance which resembles a mass of wart-like growths. This distortion of the head reduces the flexibility of the gill plates, so Lionheads require well aerated water to enable them to breathe without difficulty. The temperature of their water should be kept below 20°C (68°F), because otherwise the amount of oxygen in solution will be significantly reduced, causing them to show signs of breathing distress.

Orandas have a similar appearance to Lionheads, and probably resulted from crossings of this latter variety with Veiltails. They possess dorsal fins, unlike Lionheads, but require similar careful management. The excrescences occur more on the top of the head rather than the sides as in the case of the Lionhead. These growths can take four years to develop to their full extent.

There are various other types of ornamental goldfish which may be seen occasionally. Celestials, called 'Stargazers' by the Chinese, have their eyes positioned horizontally in their heads, so they look directly upwards. Pompons have resulted from an enlargement of the nasal septum, which partitions the nostrils. Egg-fish, first introduced to Britain from Japan in 1939, are named after the characteristic shape of their bodies. They lack dorsal fins. Some goldfish varieties are still uncommon outside China and Japan, and remain localized even there. The Pearl Scale, for example, is said to be confined largely to the province of the Kwangtung in China, but is quite readily available in Britain, although it tends to be one of the more expensive goldfish. In this instance, the scales running along the sides of the body create an illusion of pearls.

CARE OF GOLDFISH

All goldfish will thrive in an aquarium where the water temperature is maintained at about 15°C (59°F). They are active by nature, and thus require adequate swimming space, so their tank must not be cluttered with rockwork. Their movement tends to keep debris in suspension, and thus a box-type filter is recommended to keep the tank clean. Fine-leaved plants such as *Myriophyllum* will soon have their leaves covered with mulm and may well be eaten by the goldfish. *Sagittaria* and *Vallisneria* are better alternatives. Goldfish will, in fact, eat a wide variety of foodstuffs, and are not difficult to cater for, using prepared foods as a basis for their diet, augmented with suitable livefoods.

BREEDING

Goldfish in their second year are preferable for breeding purposes. They are not easy fish to sex, however, except when in breeding condition. Then, the female swells with roe and appears fatter, while the male develops white pimples on the gill plates. As many as 300 eggs can be laid in batches, which hatch in four or five days, depending on temperature. The parents should be removed after spawning, because they will often eat the eggs. If infusoria, rather than a commercial substitute, is provided at first for the young fry, a reservoir to ensure a constant supply of such food throughout the day can be easily established, using a clean rubber tube and funnel. The tube itself is tied in position as necessary, and clamped sufficiently to allow only a drop or so of the infusoria, contained in the funnel, into the tank at regular intervals. Some cannibalism may occur amongst the young fish if there is much difference in their growth rates, and only fish of similar size should be kept together in a nursery tank, taking care to avoid overcrowding them.

WHITE CLOUD MOUNTAIN MINNOW

Another cyprinid species from China, these fish were discovered in the White Cloud Mountains near Canton by a scout called Tan, and they are also known, not surprisingly, as Tan's Fish. White Cloud Mountain Minnows (*Tanichthys albonubes*) require a water temperature preferably in the range 16°–20°C (61°–68°F) and must be kept in fresh, clean water. They will give an early indication of deterioration in the water's quality by gulping at the surface, and showing signs of loss of balance.

Mountain Minnows are relatively small, being about 5 cm (2 in) in length, and are brownish-green in colour, although this fades in older specimens. Females are smaller, and have pale red lips. In a well-planted tank, they show to good effect when kept in shoals. Individual pairs can be induced to spawn by raising the water temperature to about 22°C (72°F), and providing fine-leaved plants such as *Myriophyllum*. The female does not lay a vast number of eggs, rarely more than 200, and cannibalism is unlikely to be a problem if sufficient livefood is provided. The fry are swimming freely about a week after the eggs are laid, and will breed from the age of six months onwards.

STICKLEBACKS

Various members of the family Gasterosteidae are found throughout most of Europe, extending into Asia, and even Japan, as well as North America. These fish all possess characteristic spines, ranging in number from three to fifteen, depending on the species concerned, in front of their dorsal fins. The Three-spined (*Gasterosteus aculeatus*) and Ten-spined (*Pygosteus pungitius*) occur in both fresh and brackish waters, whereas the American Four-spined Stickleback (*Apeltes quadracus*) is usually confined to brackish surroundings. These three species are most commonly seen in aquaria.

Sticklebacks have aroused considerable scientific interest, because of their unusual nesting behaviour. The reddish belly acquired by males during the breeding season has been shown to act as a challenge to any nesting males at this time. Male sticklebacks alone are responsible for constructing the hollow nests where breeding takes place. They are made from any suitable material, such as leaves or twigs, which they join together with a sticky mucus secretion. Once the nest is complete, the male forces a female into the interior, where, after a few minutes, her eggs are released and fertilized. Other females are also coerced into the nesting site, but having laid, they simply leave the eggs, which may eventually number several hundred, in the male's care. He guards the nest determinedly, driving off any potential rivals, and appears to aerate the eggs occasionally by blowing water through the nest.

As aquarium occupants, sticklebacks are aggressive and should not be housed with other coldwater species, such as goldfish, because they can inflict savage wounds with their spines. They require a tank about 60 cm (2 ft) in length, well-planted with vegetation made up of *Elodea*, *Vallisneria* and *Sagittaria*, which do well under coldwater conditions. A temperature of about 18°C (65°F) is quite suitable for these fish, and indeed they should not be exposed to temperatures over 21°C (70°F). As might be expected, sticklebacks are naturally carnivorous in their feeding habits, and should be treated accordingly, with plenty of livefood, such as whiteworm, included in their diet.

Low temperatures are necessary to bring sticklebacks into breeding condition, and during the winter, their water should be allowed to cool down as low as 5°C (41°F). One male can be kept with three or four other females in a tank, but these should be removed after they have spawned. The young fish will hatch four to seven days later, as the nest begins to disintegrate. Infusoria or fine grade egg yolk for the first couple of days are recommended, followed by brine shrimps and small daphnia, which are a favourite of all sticklebacks. Males protect their offspring for a short time after hatching. Young sticklebacks can grow to a size of about 5.25 cm (2½ in).

SUNFISHES

The sunfishes of the family Centrarchidae are natives of North America, found especially in central and eastern areas. In aquaria, they are relatively easy to cater for, but being strictly carnivorous, they will not take at all readily to inanimate prepared foods, and must be given fresh livefoods. Sunfish require slightly acid water, with a pH value of about 5, and a temperature in the range 15°–20°C (59°–68°F), which can fall slightly lower in the winter.

Over fifteen species of sunfish are known, and they will hybridize naturally in the wild. One of the most common in aquaria is the Pumpkin-seed Sunfish (*Lepomis gibbosus*) which ranges south from the Great Lakes to Florida and Texas. It is named after the characteristic appearance of the blotches on its head, and can grow to 20 cm (8 in) in size. Pygmy Sunfishes (*Elassoma evergladei*) are dwarfs in comparison, rarely attaining 2.5 cm (1 in) in length. They also have different breeding habits from other members of the family, as the female Pygmy lays in a nest, rather than in a depression created by the male fanning his fins over the substrate.

The male displays to the female, and they then move to the nesting site. The eggs are protected by the male until they hatch about three days later, and the fry remain under his care for a further week or so. They must be reared on suitable livefood, such as brine shrimps and small daphnia, from the outset. Sunfish need to be kept on their own, and even a pair may quarrel amongst themselves, so a planted environment, giving some cover, is recommended. They are not easy to sex outside the breeding season, until the male becomes more colourful.

Pumpkin-seed Sunfish (*Lepomis gibbosus*).

PART II

THE TROPICAL MARINE AQUARIUM

9 SETTING UP THE MARINE AQUARIUM

Early attempts at keeping marine fish were made during Victorian times, using fish caught in coastal waters, but they proved largely unsuccessful. There were no saltwater substitutes, nor any of the other equipment which is available today. Serious interest in the maintenance of marine fish as a decorative feature in the home began in earnest during the 1950s, being kindled by the unusual, colourful and often bizarre fish which were being imported from the coral reefs of the world. At this time, however, the requirements of the fish were not fully appreciated, and the technology available to care for them was still rather limited.

Since then, however, considerable advances have been made, and a suitable environment for such fish can be created without too much difficulty. There has also been increasing interest in the various invertebrate creatures which are now quite widely available, although their requirements may well differ from those of the fish. Indeed, some marine aquarists have tanks containing a selection of invertebrates such as sea anemones and corals, with relatively few, if any, fish present.

The keeping of marine creatures in aquaria remains a relatively expensive hobby, compared to a freshwater set-up. The cost of equipment, as well as of the ultimate inhabitants for the tank, is not cheap, and incidental running costs such as lighting can mount up, depending on the species being maintained. In addition, there is little likelihood of producing home-bred fish that can be sold to offset costs, since marines rarely reproduce successfully under aquarium conditions. Provided that these points are appreciated, however, the unique beauty provided by a marine tank is more than adequate compensation.

MARINE TANKS

Before the advent of silicone rubber sealant for tank building purposes, it proved very difficult to construct suitable aquaria for marine species, because of the highly corrosive properties of seawater. Metal-frame tanks should never be used, and even those designed with stainless steel will be attacked by the salt. It did prove possible to coat exposed metalwork with an inert, protective substance such as epoxy resin. Asbestos cement tanks were also tried; these had one pane of glass, at the front, and were exceptionally heavy even when empty.

Today, it is a matter of deciding between a glass tank, sealed with silicone rubber, or a plastic unit. The former type is usually preferable, since the drawbacks associated with the use of plastic tanks for freshwater fish still apply if they are used to house marine life. Their sides discolour and scratch easily, and many are too small. A large tank, at least 90 cm (3 ft) in length, 30 cm (1 ft) wide and 38 cm (15 in) deep, should be acquired for marine fish.

A plastic hood to fit the tank is often recommended, because if a metal hood is used, it will have to be painted with an undercoat and a good gloss top coat. The paint will serve to protect the metal from accidental splashing. Droplets of water will corrode the metal, and once chemicals, such as aluminium, get into the aquarium water, they are likely to poison its inhabitants. Wooden hoods, constructed of a white laminate on the inside, to act as a light reflector, can also be used. The type of hood may be affected by the filtration system: the Tunze system, for example, requires a relatively tall covering above the aquarium.

The water temperature will need to be kept constant, within the usual range of 24°–26.5°C (75°–80°F), which necessitates a heater of the appropriate wattage, operating under the control of a thermostat. Equipment of this type that is stoppered by means of rubber coverings should not be used in a marine tank, because this barrier will be attacked by the salinity and perish, destroying the unit as a result. Heaters and thermostats with nylon filaments are marketed to overcome this difficulty. A thermometer will again be required to keep a check on the temperature of the water.

It does not matter if a marine tank receives a certain amount of direct sunlight; this will stimulate algal growth and assist in the care of invertebrates. The exposure and intensity of lighting depends on the individual occupants of the tank. Fluorescent tubes are normally used for marine aquaria containing fish. It is preferable to acquire one of the types which possess a light spectrum resembling that of natural daylight. They are sold in various lengths, and should run nearly the full length of the tank. As a refinement, some fluorescent tubes incorporate a power twist, which, the manufacturers claim, gives about 10 per cent extra output of light compared to a normal tube of the same length and wattage. The efficiency of these tube lights gradually decreases, however, and a spare should always be kept handy. It is likely in most cases that two or more tubes will be required, and to get maximum benefit from them, the reflector in the hood must be efficient. A white gloss paint should therefore be used if necessary over this surface.

In order to prevent droplets of water settling on the lights, a plastic splash shield with perforations should be placed between the light and the water, across the top of the tank. When high intensity lighting is required, in aquaria containing anemones, for example, a mercury vapour lamp should be used to provide an additional light source. These give out an intense bright light, yet do not produce a lot of heat. They can be directed over particular parts of an aquarium, where an anemone is sited, but can be difficult to accommodate under a standard hood. In the wild, fish are rarely exposed to conditions of total darkness, and a low wattage night light, such as a small 15W bulb, can prove a useful investment, helping to prevent panic among the aquarium occupants with the resulting risk of losses.

WATER PURIFICATION AND AERATION

An adequate filtration system is vital for the average marine tank. The coral reefs where the majority of the fish and invertebrates occur are extremely stable biological environments, and their lifeforms are correspondingly sensitive to poor water quality. The same principles of filtration apply in the case of the marine set-up as for a freshwater aquarium. Undergravel filters, covering the whole of the floor, are a popular choice for many marine tanks, since they are cheap, require relatively little maintenance and prove quite adaptable. A layer of cockle shell with coral sand on top is a typical combination for use on

Substrate filtration with the water moving upwards through the substrate.

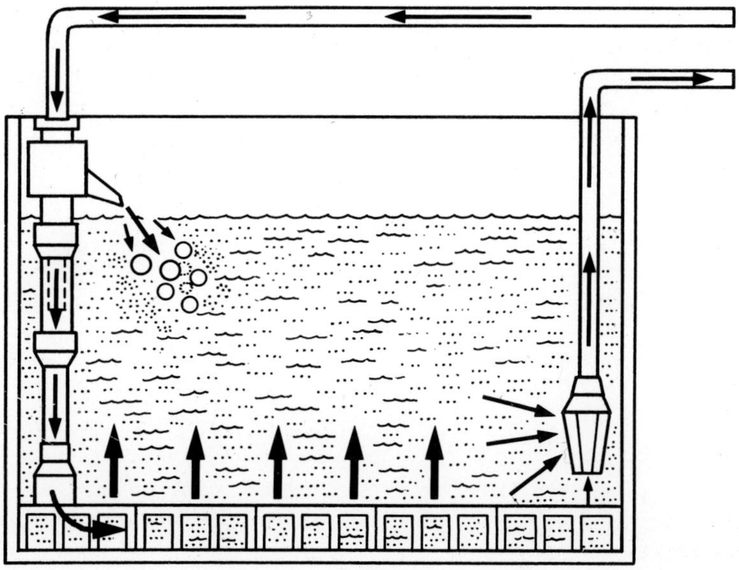

the aquarium floor, above an under-gravel filter. An average depth of about 7.5 cm (3 in) is used. The practice of placing filter wool immediately over the filter is now rarely seen. It was thought to help the efficiency of the system, but in reality proved impossible to keep clean without disturbing the whole tank.

As an adjunct to an under-gravel filter, a standard box-type unit can prove beneficial, especially once the aquarium has matured. It is important to use a marine charcoal, whose active surface area may be in excess of 1000 sq m per g, thus proving more efficient than standard filter charcoal, whose activity is often only a quarter of this figure. This kind of filtration system is sometimes described as being 'semi-natural'. A slightly different method, relying on an under-gravel filter in combination with a power filter, has become increasingly popular with marine aquarists during recent years. It is known as the reverse-flow under-gravel system. The power filter itself incorporates both a pump and a filtration chamber containing marine charcoal, filter wool and coral sand. Water from the tank passes through this unit first, and is re-introduced to the aquarium by being forced under the filter bed of the under-gravel filter. It thus passes up through the substrate into the tank, which is the reverse of the more widely-used method of down-flow under-gravel filtration. The reverse-flow system is a more efficient means of removing waste matter from the aquarium, since passage of the water through the power filter initially takes out debris which would otherwise accumulate in the covering on the aquarium floor. Biological filtration is not compromised, and the beneficial aerobic bacteria will continue to work in association with the under-gravel filter.

Power filters can be used independently of an under-gravel unit, but normally have to be operated with other equipment to maintain the water's quality. The size of power filter will depend in turn on the water volume in the aquarium. They are relatively quiet when operating, but expensive to purchase in the first instance. Some power filters only contain a plastic foam sponge, and thus act on the basis of mechanical filtration, since no carbon is present. A power filter containing filter media as described previously is a much better purchase.

The 'sterile system' based on the use of a power filter, is often re-inforced with a protein skimmer, and other apparatus which has been devised with the primary aim of destroying any pathogens present in the water. Polluted water will produce foam containing the waste matter when it is mixed with air. The protein skimmer utilizes this principle, by taking

A protein skimmer helps to remove organic waste from the aquarium water.

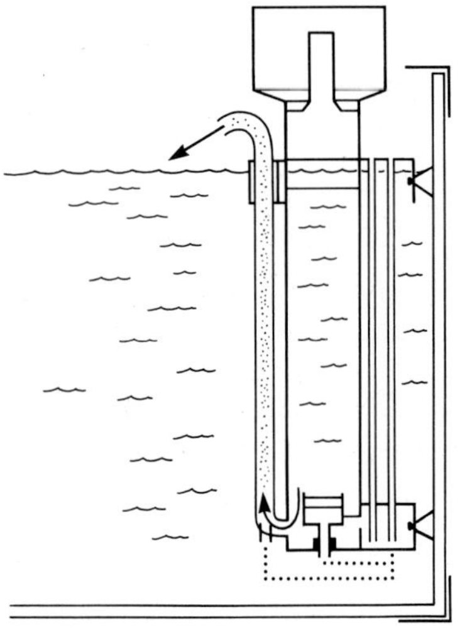

An ozonizer produces a mixture of ozone and air.

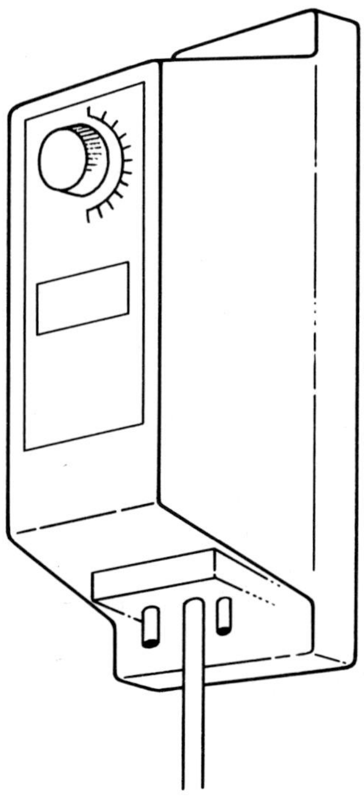

Amphiprion frenatus in a sea-anemone.

Amphiprion ephippium in a sea-anemone.

An attractive group of corals and small tubeworms.

water from the tank, aerating it and retaining the foam in a separate container which must be emptied regularly. This system is of particular value in removing organic waste, and useful in aquaria containing occupants such as triggerfish, which are naturally messy fish.

An ozonizer is frequently run in conjunction with a protein skimmer, and may increase its efficiency three-fold. This equipment produces the gas ozone, by means of electric sparks being passed through air, which contains oxygen. Ozone (O_3) is a condensed form of oxygen (O_2) which has sterilizing properties. It is not only capable of killing potential disease-causing organisms, but is also able to convert both ammonia and nitrite into nitrate. The ozone can be liberated into the protein skimmer, or passed into the tank, where a diffuser will help to maximize its effect. By producing small bubbles of the gas, its overall surface area will be increased, thus maximizing its contact with water and molecules in the aquarium, which it can neutralize.

Another piece of apparatus, useful for improving the condition of the water, as well as controlling the spread of disease, is a diatom filter. It is similar in its mode of action to a power filter, but the medium in this instance is so fine that it can extract particles only a micron ($^1/_{1,000,000}$ m) in diameter from the water, so that various disease-causing organisms will actually be retained in this filter. As might be expected, however, its efficiency is soon compromised so it cannot be left operating for long periods.

The ultra-violet sterilizer is, like ozonizers, relatively expensive, and while it may prove beneficial in certain circumstances, it should not be considered an essential purchase from the outset. The ultra-violet light itself, produced within the sealed cover, acts as a sterilizing agent on microbes present in the water, which is pumped through the chamber. In theory, this is an effective method, but in practice, the lethal effects of the radiation decline quite rapidly once the unit is being used, as the output of ultra-violet light falls. The water in turn cannot be exposed for a sufficiently long period of time for maximum efficiency. An ultra-violet sterilizer is not recommended for aquaria containing invertebrates, which are filter-feeders, since it may, especially when new, make the water too sterile for them.

The latest significant innovation in the filtration of marine tanks is the Tunze system. It is expensive, but especially for larger tanks, containing in excess of 455 l (100 gal), the cost involved compares favourably with the outlay required for alternative methods of filtration. The unit itself fits into the roof of the tank, necessitating a relatively high wooden hood. Being located in this position, maintenance can be carried out very easily, with minimum disturbance to the aquarium itself. The Tunze system is generally comprised of two pre-filters, through which water from the tank is drawn. The majority of this then goes back into the tank via an outlet close to the adjoining pump. The remainder passes over the four biological trickle filters, before re-entering the aquarium. In terms of maintenance of the unit itself, only the pre-filters need cleaning, every fortnight or so. The use of a protein skimmer with this system is recommended, and if necessary, its motor could be used to substitute for that of the filter pump. Stockists of the Tunze system often quote for the whole aquarium, including the hood if required, and this is normally the most economical means of purchasing it.

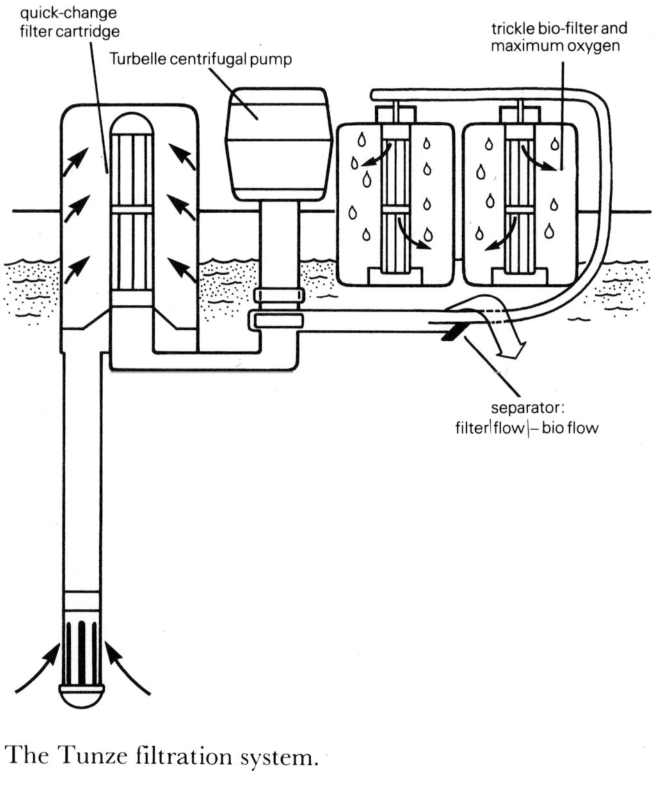

The Tunze filtration system.

While saltwater cannot absorb as much atmospheric oxygen as freshwater, the oxygen requirement of marine creatures is much higher than that of freshwater species. The choice of a reliable and sufficiently powerful air pump is thus of prime importance. In many cases where a filter is present in the tank, no separate aeration system will be necessary, as movement of water through the filter produces adequate aeration. Where additional oxygenation of the water is required, this can be achieved by means of an air-stone, run off the filtration system, or under the control of another air pump. Marine fish live in a naturally turbulent environment, and movement of water in the aquarium via a power filter will help to mimic the effect of waves.

In the case of invertebrates, it can be possible to keep them successfully without any form of filter, although aeration must be provided. Described as the 'natural system', this method relies entirely on bacteria in the tank to degrade toxic substances present in solution, while filter-feeders such as sponges are largely responsible for removing solid particulate matter. Although the system obviously decreases the costs involved in setting up the aquarium, it is fraught with difficulties. The biological balance is of necessity very fine, and losses are likely to occur with any build-up of nitrite or related compounds. In order to achieve any measure of success, the stocking rate must be kept extremely low. Very few fishes can be included, as a tank of this type will probably support less than one quarter of the population that could be kept in a filtered aquarium of identical dimensions. This clearly detracts from the appeal of such a set-up, which has no realistic advantages over the semi-natural or sterile systems of management already outlined.

SETTING UP AND FILLING THE TANK

The tank will first need to be washed out thoroughly, as described in the freshwater section, and positioned on a firm base with an intervening layer of expanded polystyrene. The under-gravel filter, with all holes open, should next be put in place and covered with a layer of cockle shell, with coral sand over it, especially if detritus-feeding invertebrates, such as starfish, will ultimately be housed in the aquarium. These creatures move over the floor, filtering the sand for any traces of food, and will not readily accept coarser substitutes. Certain fish, such as wrasses, will bury themselves in the substrate and coral sand will enable them to do this without difficulty. This top layer should again be contoured, running down to the front of the tank, so any debris such as uneaten food can be seen and removed easily, before it pollutes the tank. An aquarium cleaner, running on batteries, is a useful acquisition for this purpose, causing minimal disturbance to the tank and its occupants when in use.

Seawater itself is not sufficiently pure for a marine tank housing creatures from coral reefs, and obviously in many areas, collection would present almost insurmountable difficulties. An artificial substitute can be prepared by adding the appropriate quantity of synthetic sea salt to a given volume of water, bearing in mind the tank's capacity. Trace elements should also be included in the sea salt mixture, although they may alternatively need to be added separately, being sold for mixing with the synthetic salt in solution. They are chemicals present in minute amounts in ordinary seawater which prove of particular importance in ensuring the overall health of the aquarium's inhabitants. Other chemicals, such as vitamins and various growth substances, are also included in some mixtures. Use of a pre-matured salt will enable a tank to be set up more quickly, since the maturation process is speeded up considerably.

You can mix the salt most conveniently once the tank is about half-full. Tip the required quantity of sea salts for the tank into the clean plastic bucket being used to fill the aquarium. Then add water, from the coldwater supply as usual to minimize the risk of introducing excessive copper from the heating system and pipework. Stir the salt round in the bucket so that the majority dissolves, before pouring it into the tank. Top up the water level to a point which will allow the addition of pieces of rockwork and other decoration.

Next, fit the heater and thermostat, along with any other filters which are to be used, and switch on the apparatus so that the water will gradually warm up. The water will benefit from aeration for a day or so, to ensure that the salts are completely dissolved. After this period, check the water's chemistry, using the appropriate tests. For pH, a sample of water can be drawn off by means of a pipette and added to the tube with the indicator solution as instructed. It will be on the alkaline side of the scale, normally in the range of 7.8 to 8.4 and an accurate reading will be made possible by a distinctive alteration in the colour of the indicator. Readings should always be made under conditions of natural light as far as possible.

In the case of a marine aquarium, the specific gravity (SG) or density of the water is important, being a reflection of the concentration of dissolved salts present. It is measured by means of an instrument called a hydrometer, which is calibrated to function at a particular water temperature. The sample to be tested must therefore be at this figure for maximum accuracy, since the density will fall with an increase in temperature. The specific gravity reading for seawater is normally in the range of 1.020 to 1.022, but can vary slightly in certain areas, being higher in Caribbean waters, where an SG of 1.025 may be anticipated. Most tropical marine fish require water with an SG of the order of 1.023, which will have a salinity (or salt content) of 35 parts per thousand. If a much higher figure is recorded, this is likely to prove harmful for invertebrates in the first instance. Evaporation leads to a loss of water, thus causing an increase in the salinity of the remaining water in the tank. In order to correct this, only ordinary, aged water at the correct temperature, and not additional seawater, should be added, otherwise the salinity will continue to rise unchecked. As salinity increases, so the oxygen content of the water falls, at any given temperature.

In a newly-established tank, it will take several days for the SG reading to stabilize, once the salts have been dissolved. Alterations to the SG at this stage can be made by adding more of the synthetic salt mixture, or alternatively, diluting the solution with more tapwater, as required. The appetite of the fish is likely to be poor in an aquarium with a lower SG than normal, although there is evidence to suggest their lifespan may be extended, as their metabolic rate is slowed.

Relationship between temperature, salinity and density of sea water

Temperature in C										
20	1.0193	1.0200	1.0208	1.0215	1.0223	1.0231	1.0239	1.0246	1.0253	1.0259
21	1.0191	1.0198	1.0206	1.0214	1.0221	1.0229	1.0237	1.0244	1.0251	1.0258
22	1.0189	1.0197	1.0204	1.0212	1.0219	1.0227	1.0235	1.0242	1.0249	1.0256
23	1.0187	1.0195	1.0202	1.0210	1.0217	1.0224	1.0232	1.0240	1.0248	1.0254
24	1.0184	1.0193	1.0200	1.0207	1.0215	1.0222	1.0230	1.0238	1.0245	1.0252
25	1.0182	1.0190	1.0197	1.0205	1.0213	1.0220	1.0228	1.0235	1.0242	1.0250
26	1.0179	1.0187	1.0194	1.0202	1.0210	1.0217	1.0224	1.0232	1.0239	1.0247
27	1.0175	1.0184	1.0191	1.0199	1.0206	1.0213	1.0221	1.0229	1.0237	1.0243
28	1.0172	1.0180	1.0188	1.0195	1.0203	1.0210	1.0218	1.0225	1.0233	1.0240
29	1.0169	1.0176	1.0184	1.0192	1.0200	1.0207	1.0214	1.0221	1.0229	1.0237
30	1.0165	1.0172	1.0180	1.0188	1.0195	1.0202	1.0210	1.0217	1.0225	1.0233
Salinity in parts per thousand	**28**	**29**	**30**	**31**	**32**	**33**	**34**	**35**	**36**	**37**

Oxygen in cc per litre

Temperature in C	**Density** (approx.)	1.0225	1.0245	1.0255
10		6.54	6.46	6.37
15		5.94	5.87	5.80
20		5.44	5.38	5.31
25		4.99	4.94	4.85
30		4.56	4.50	4.44

DECORATION IN THE MARINE TANK

Care must be taken when aquascaping a marine tank to ensure that the items used are not likely to lower the pH reading. In the way of rockwork, hard limestones are preferable, and these can be obtained from dealers if necessary. Westmoreland is a popular choice, while slate can also be used to construct hiding places within the tank. Rockwork must be washed off very thoroughly, to remove any dirt, before it is placed in the tank. Dead corals of various shapes and shells can be used to create the appearance of a miniature reef. It is vital that these are cleaned thoroughly before use, so that decaying matter will not be introduced into the aquarium with them. Coral polyps are living creatures which erect hard, calcareous exoskeletons around themselves. Although coral may appear clean and white when purchased, it must be sterilized to remove any remaining trace of its former occupants. Immerse the pieces in a strong solution of bleach for at least a week, and then wash them off very thoroughly, until no trace of the smell of the bleach can be detected. Dead coral is usually white, but occasionally may be dyed artificially. Such pieces should not be used in a marine tank, as they may prove hazardous to its occupants. A few hard coral exoskeletons can be coloured even when dead, such as the red of the Organ-pipe Coral (*Tubipora*). Soft forms of coral are also available, but these are more difficult to prepare for the aquarium, and perhaps are not as attractive as their hard counterparts.

Shells need similar treatment to coral before they can be placed safely in the tank. Those obtained from bivalve molluscs are easier to clean, since they are usually cleaved in half. In contrast, the interiors of the attractive cowrie shells are relatively inaccessible, and bleach will certainly be required to remove any organic material which may still be present within.

These inert tank decorations can be put into the tank before it has matured; however, 'living' rock must be introduced later. Chunks are collected in the wild, and are therefore teeming with minute living organisms which help to populate the aquarium once it has been set up. Rockwork of this type will be of great value in establishing many marine invertebrates. The holes in 'living rock' provide natural hiding places for various creatures, such as crustaceans and sea-squirts. In the aquarium, it will help to keep the pH of the water stable.

A 'living rock' from the Mediterranean.

PLANTS

In contrast to most freshwater aquaria, marine tanks appear to be rather lacking in plant life. This is because few recognizable plants are found in the vicinity of coral reefs, but it is possible to use artificial

Caulerpa racemosa.

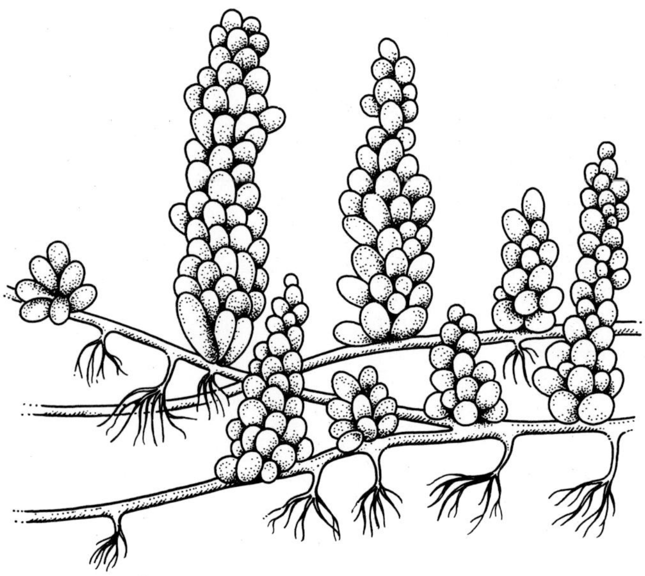

The green algae *Caulerpa prolifera* is the species that lives best in a marine aquarium.

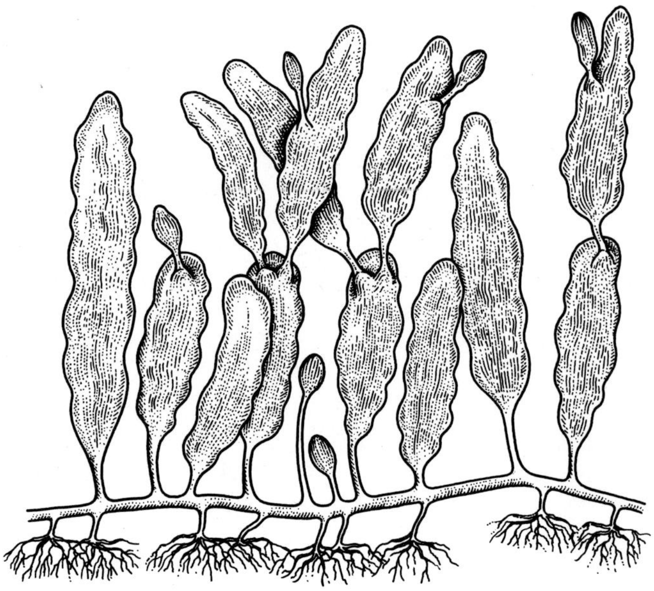

Caulerpa sertularioides.

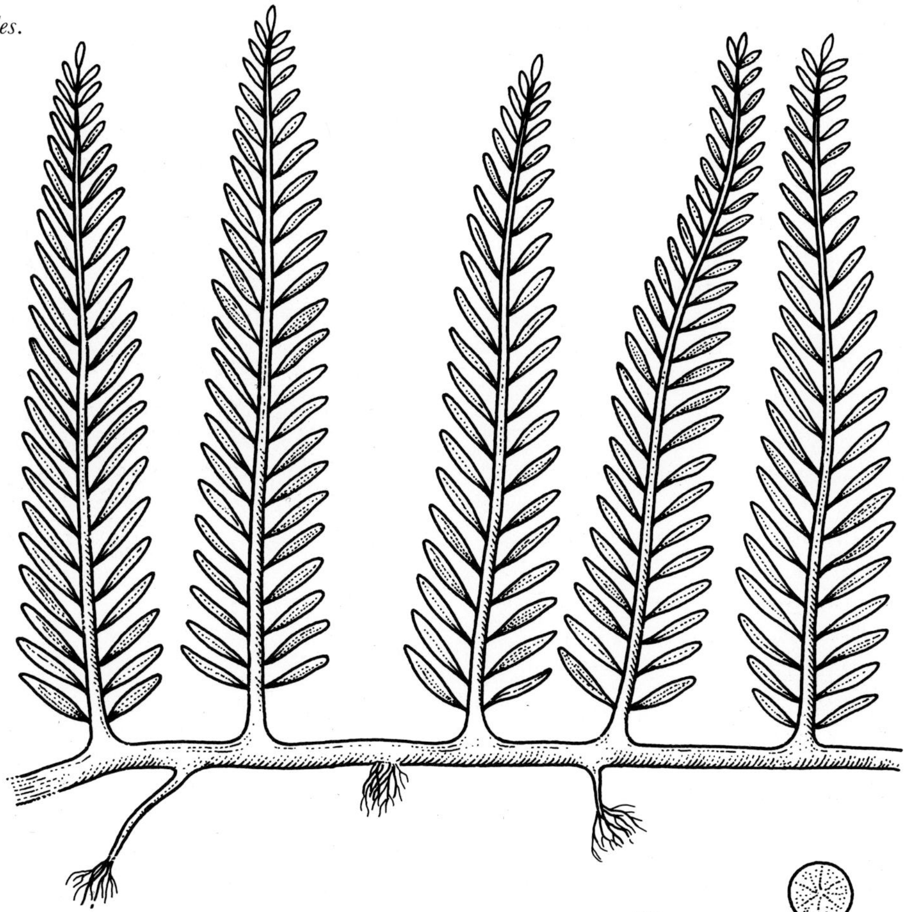

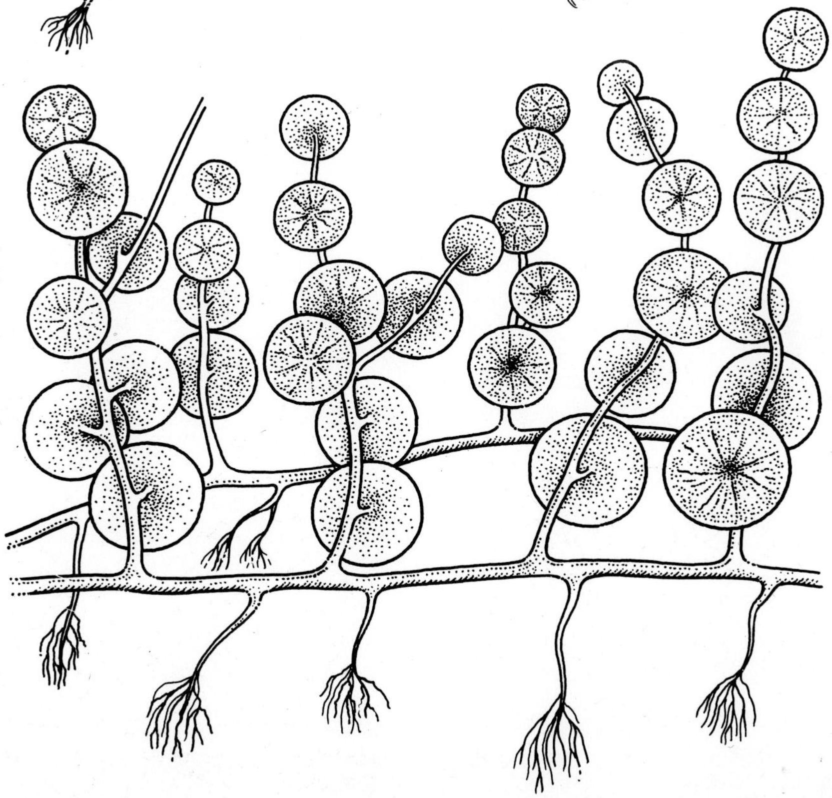

Caulerpa macrodisca.

Maturation of a marine aquarium

1. 'Natural' maturation

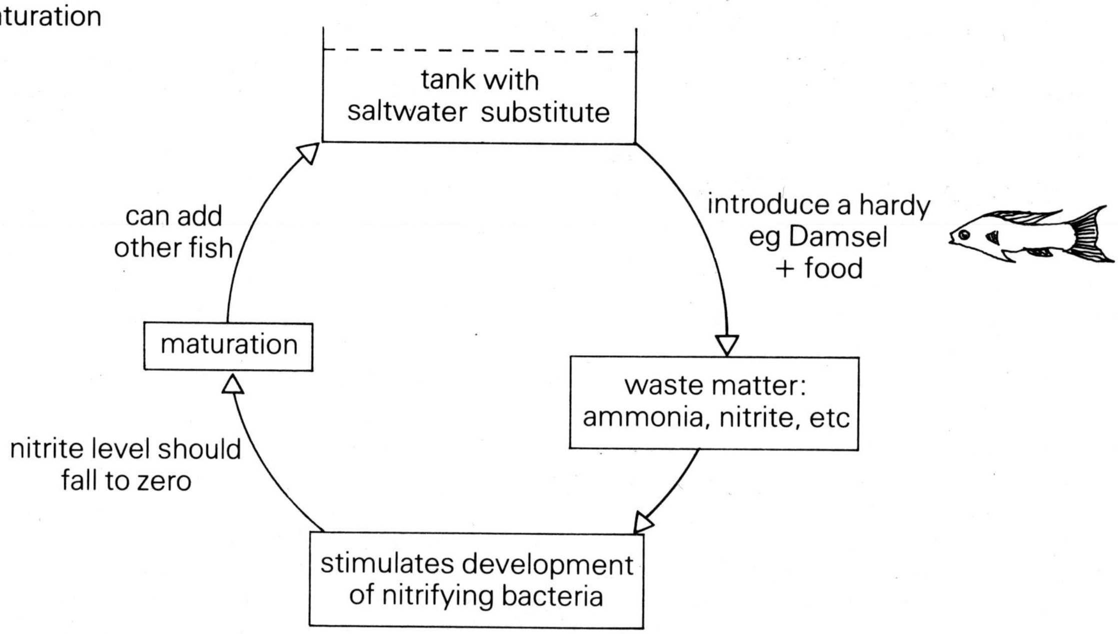

2. 'Artificial' maturation

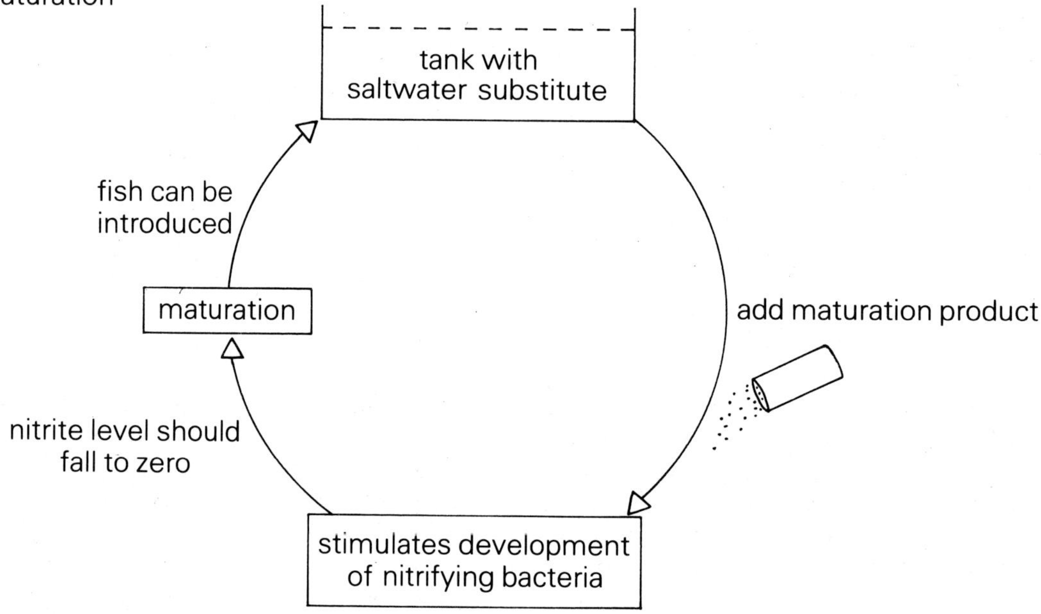

Advantages:
1. Quicker.
2. Entails no initial commitment at the outset to hardy, nitrite-tolerant fish, which are liable to prove aggressive later to other, more sensitive fish.

Note: *An aquarium for invertebrates only can be matured by similar means. Many aquarists in this instance still follow the 'natural' system, introducing nitrite-tolerant creatures, such as hermit crabs, in the first instance. Overcrowding at this stage must be avoided at all costs.*

plants if desired. The more advanced forms of alga can be cultured successfully if they are not destroyed by the fish. *Caulerpa* species are commonly available, and produce leaf-like fronds. They spread in the tank by means of stolons, pushing down roots when they come into contact with a suitable anchorage. The shape of the fronds can be quite variable; *C. prolifera*, for example, produces strap-like fronds, while those of *C. sertulariordes* are finer. Other decorative algae which are often available include Shaving Brush (*Penicillus*) and the Sea-cactus (*Haliomeda*). These algae will grow better in the aquarium if they are purchased already established on rocks.

It is important to check that the SG readings are compatible before moving algae to a new tank, otherwise they will be destroyed before they can establish themselves. Apart from photosynthesizing, algae provide a valuable service by utilizing nitrate, as well as other nutrients present in the water, forming protein which in turn will be consumed by the tank's other inhabitants. For this reason, other less conspicuous forms of algae should also be encouraged. Brown algae are often the first form to be seen in a newly-established tank, utilizing silicon for their growth. Other types of algae may be green or blue in colour, while an attractive red form can also be cultured. Marine algae require good periods of illumination if they are to develop and thrive. Preparations are available, which should be added to the tank in order to stimulate algal growth, but they will not substitute for adequate lighting.

CHEMICAL MATURATION

Once the aquarium is filled, the water may be ready for fish and other higher forms of marine life, but the aquarium itself will need to be matured to cope with their waste products. The process of maturation can be speeded up considerably by using a pre-matured synthetic salt as discussed previously. As an alternative, with a traditional artificial salt, the growth of the essential bacteria for nitrification purposes will be significantly improved by adding a maturation product. The length of time required will be partially influenced by the floor covering of the aquarium, since the bacteria prefer coral sand and cockle shell as a growing medium.

The maturation product contains both bacteria and essential nutrients for them. A small quantity is generally added on a daily basis, its effects being monitored by means of nitrite tests. Once a peak nitrite figure of 15 ppm is reached, no further concentrate need be added. The level of nitrite falls, as it is converted to nitrate by the developing colony of bacteria. When no nitrite can be detected in the tank, the process of maturation is virtually complete. The length of time taken can be quite variable, but it is likely to be of the order of two or three weeks. Keeping the tank well-illuminated and aerated will reduce this period; and the addition of some coral sand from an existing, healthy tank once the nitrite level has risen to 15 ppm, thus introducing additional bacteria, can also be beneficial.

The pH must be checked at this stage, and should be in the region of 8.0 to 8.4. If it has fallen below 8.0, then partially change the water, replacing about a quarter of the tank's total volume with a freshly-made solution of saltwater. Once the pH has stabilized at the desired level, and the SG is also satisfactory, you can introduce some hardy fish into the tank, along with chunks of 'living rock' if desired. Any decorative algae should be put in place before the fish are obtained, so that they have an opportunity to take root, maximizing the likelihood of their becoming established.

EARLY STOCKING OF THE AQUARIUM

Fish differ in their relative sensitivities to nitrite, and amongst the hardy species are various damsels and targetfish (*Therapon jarbua*). It is important to check beforehand that the pH and SG where the fish are held approximate as closely as possible to those in the new tank to which they will be transferred. As an additional precaution, a suitable preventive treatment for Velvet Disease, caused by the protozoal parasite *Oodinium*, should be added to the tank. Care must be taken when selecting such preparations, however, since many remedies for marine ailments are unsuitable for use in tanks destined to hold invertebrates, and filtration over carbon may also inactivate them. Outbreaks of Velvet Disease, with correspondingly high mortality, are almost inevitable under conditions of stress and relatively high nitrite levels, as occur when fish are used to mature a fresh aquarium.

The stocking ratio should be kept low in the early stages, allowing 2.5 cm (1 in) of fish to 18 l (4 gal) of water for the first six months or so, after which it can be raised if desired to a maximum of 2.5 cm (1 in) per 9 l (2 gal). It is often best to include only a few hardy fish at first, rather than filling the aquarium completely, which will effectively prevent the introduction of other, more sensitive species later.

Care must be taken to ensure that species are compatible, and smaller specimens are generally preferable for this reason. Unfortunately, many of the species recommended for the early stocking of a marine aquarium are both territorial and aggressive by nature. The Mono (*Monodactylus argenteus*) is an exception, being both hardy and peaceful. The selection of single individuals of each species tends to reduce the risk of bullying, and subsequent losses. Individual fish vary in temperament, however, so statements of compatibility can prove to be erroneous.

In the case of an aquarium intended for invertebrates only, nitrite-tolerant creatures, such as crustaceans and molluscs, should be introduced initially, before filter and detritus feeders. They will help to ensure the development of nitrifying bacteria, since, in view of their grosser feeding habits, they produce more waste products, in the form of ammonia which the bacteria will utilize. Once the nitrite reading is zero, the environment will be ready to support other, more vulnerable invertebrates.

When transferring a marine creature from one environment to another, every effort should be made to keep the stress down to a minimum. For this reason, the lights above an aquarium need to be switched off immediately before the plastic bag containing the creature is allowed to float on the surface of the water. By this means, the water temperature in the bag will gradually rise over the course of twenty minutes or so and then the fish can be allowed out. It will often retreat at first to the nearest available cover, but should soon venture out.

FEEDING AND GENERAL AQUARIUM MAINTENANCE

Any food left uneaten in the aquarium will be a serious pollutant, serving to raise the nitrite level, perhaps with catastrophic consequences. Just sufficient food should be supplied to satisfy the appetites of the tank's inhabitants within a quarter of an hour of being introduced. Certain species are relatively slow feeders and must be given an opportunity to acquire their share when in the company of more rapacious individuals. Formerly, foodstuffs of marine origin obtained from fishmongers were often used, yet presented a constant threat of disease. With the advent of specially prepared foods for marine fish, their care has become free of such hazards, while remaining relatively straightforward. A combination of dried food, with a variety of the various irradiated foodstuffs, is recommended as a basic diet.

The majority of marine fish consume vegetable matter as part of their food intake, and certain fish, such as Tangs, will naturally eat quite large quantities of algae. Their diet may need to be supplemented accordingly, with vegetable matter such as chopped dandelion, or a dry substitute if there is insufficient algae in the tank. In order to encourage the appetite of new arrivals or sick fish, a vitamin supplement for marine life should be added to the water in the aquarium. Regular use of such a product will provide a general tonic for the inhabitants of an established tank. Livefood may prove necessary for fish which are otherwise reluctant to eat, although inanimate foodstuffs can be waved in front of them, stimulating the natural movement of potential prey, by attaching a portion to a piece of string. Brine shrimps are the only suitable livefood for marine species - daphnia, for example, will die rapidly in saltwater, and then pollute the aquarium. A constant supply of brine shrimps will be essential if seahorses are to be maintained successfully. Invertebrates, such as crustaceans and sea anemones, will take food intended for fish, but special complete foods will be required by filter-feeders. This can also be useful for rearing fry of marine fish.

The main danger period in the life of the aquarium occurs once the first fish have been introduced. It is advisable to check the nitrite level on a daily basis at first. Provided that no uneaten food is left to decompose and the tank is matured and not overstocked, this figure should not go above 0 ppm. To distinguish between nitrite and nitrate requires two tests, the nitrite test being undertaken first. It now appears that nitrate itself can have a detrimental effect on the health of marine creatures, depending on the concentration and the particular species concerned. *Octopus* species and living corals are very sensitive and do not tolerate nitrate levels above 20 ppm, while for other more hardy marine species, the level should not be allowed to rise above 50 ppm.

Specific gravity and pH readings can be taken perhaps twice a week. Where the pH shows signs of falling, then a saltwater buffer solution should be obtained, to compensate both for cationic and anionic loss. The time for a partial water change will come when the effects of the buffer solution last only for a matter of hours. Replacement of perhaps a quarter of the water in the aquarium will be necessary. It should be warmed up with a separate heater before being introduced carefully, by syphoning or very gently pouring so as not to disturb the tank more than necessary.

Salt will crystallize out around the tank, with water being lost by evaporation, affecting the specific gravity as a result. Fresh, not salt, water is required in this instance. Over a period of time, the trace elements present in the original water will have been utilized by the tank's inhabitants. This loss can be compensated for by the addition of a further supply, given in small amounts on a weekly basis, after the aquarium has been set up for at least a month. Addition of algal and vitamin tonics at the same time can also be beneficial to all the tank's inhabitants. Many of these products must be stored in the dark to retain their efficiency over a period of time.

The box or power filter will need its constituents replaced, with the actual interval being dependent on various factors. Dirty water, with yellowish coloration is a sign that the charcoal is becoming deactivated. The under-gravel filter can be left undisturbed for a long time, providing it does not become clogged with debris. When a tank does have to be emptied completely, then all the tank decorations should be removed first, which will make it easier to catch the fish, and there is less risk of injuring them in the process.

BREEDING MARINE FISH IN AQUARIA

The majority of species cannot be sexed by visual means, but a pair may well split off from a group when spawning is imminent. Much still remains to be learnt about the breeding of marine fish, but light has been shown to be an important trigger for conditioning purposes in certain cases. Clownfish can be encouraged to spawn by adopting a lighting regimen giving sixteen hours of illumination per day. The eggs of some species float, and in the confines of an aquarium, they will be easy prey for the tank's occupants. A separate tank will thus be required, to maximize the chances of success.

Once the fry hatch, the rearing system employed at the National Marine Fisheries Service Beaufort Laboratory in North Carolina, where a number of species have been reared successfully, relies on a bare environment, with black plastic being used to line the nursery quarters. This encourages the fry to congregate in the centre of the tank, near the surface. The water is treated with an antibiotic to decrease the risk of pathogens becoming established and destroying the baby fish. Brine shrimp nauplii are too large as a first food for many fry, and as an alternative, the minute rotifer *Brachionus plicatilus* is used. These tiny organisms feed on marine algae, and have to be separated by means of filtration. Two sieves, made with mesh 0.30 mm and 0.06 mm diameter, as used for plankton nets, are required for this purpose. As a ready alternative, a double layer of plain cotton handkerchiefs, free of contamination from washing powders, can be used for the same purpose. Coarse debris will be kept above, while water and algal cells will flow right through, leaving *Brachionus* trapped in between the two layers, ready to be fed to the fry.

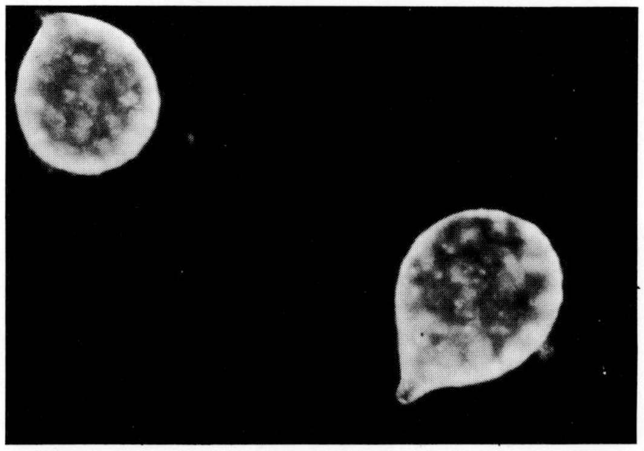

Individual parasites of *Oodinium ocellatum*, × 250.

There is, at present, no commercially prepared food of this type, but balanced foods intended for filter-feeding invertebrates can be offered to fry several days after hatching. Brine shrimp nauplii are suitable for fry of some species within two days, and should be accepted by all fry once they reach the age of a fortnight. Gentle aeration of the water in the tank should begin at this stage. For marine aquarists who are particularly interested in breeding fish, probably Blennies, Gobies, Cardinalfish and Seahorses offer the greatest possibilities.

DISEASES

Once the aquarium and its occupants are established, the likelihood of disease suddenly appearing is relatively slight. Environmental triggers, such as high levels of nitrite, can be detected in many instances. The most significant disease caused by *Oodinium* has been mentioned previously in this context. Velvet Disease and other parasitic infections can be reliably eliminated by means of a suitable proprietary remedy, taking care to avoid copper-based treatments for tanks housing invertebrates in the company of fish. Amongst other protozoal parasites, a ciliate species,

Cryptocarion irritans, causes white spot in marine fish. Seahorses can be prone to this infection. Treatment as for *Oodinium* should prove effective. It will also act against *Benedenia* which is a fluke infestation concentrated at first around the eyes. *Pomacanthus* species appear especially susceptible, with an affected fish showing an aversion to light, and the eyes themselves become cloudy. Swollen eyes can also result from a bacterial infection, and are often indicative of a deterioration in the quality of the water.

Oodinium ocellatum. A later stage of division, × 420.

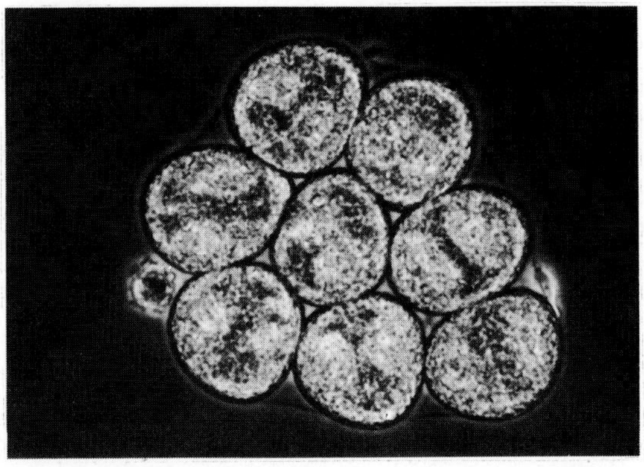

Fin-rot may occur in marine fish, and the fins themselves are the first site where the signs of the viral disease, lymphocystis, may be apparent. This can resolve itself once the fish has settled down in a new environment. The creamy swellings in some cases may have to be cut away though, with a sharp pair of scissors, leaving healthy surrounding tissue intact as far as possible. A suitable treatment must then be added to the water to prevent the risk of secondary infections developing at the site.

Marine fish do not suffer as much from fungal disease as their freshwater counterparts, however, although *Ichthyosporidium hoferi* infections are serious. This is a fungus which develops within the body, especially in *Centropyge* species, causing abdominal swelling and protruding eyes. No treatment is effective for such cases.

10 MARINE FISH

A large selection of marine fish are imported annually, and the following section covers many of the more common and hardy species, arranged in family groupings. In most areas of the country, there are specialist dealers in marine fish, who often advertise in the fish-keeping journals. Specialist equipment, and other items, such as rotifer cultures, can be obtained direct or possibly by mail order from them. A general aquarist store will alternatively be able to order equipment or particular fish if required, but this can work out more expensive. It is useful to know the scientific name of a species when making an enquiry, because common names are quite variable and a supplier will be assisted in sending the desired fish if this information is provided. Although fish can be dispatched by rail, it is much better to collect them personally whenever possible.

The supply of marine fish and invertebrates can be quite variable, depending on factors such as the time of year, since they are almost all imported, from centres such as the Philippines, Hawaii and Singapore. It is generally preferable to opt for a small to medium-size specimen. Larger fish command higher prices, and yet, being older, have a proportionately lower life expectancy. Given adequate care, most marine fish will grow well in an aquarium, and the growth rate can be quite spectacular in certain cases, such as Batfish. Younger specimens in many instances also have more attractive markings, and often feed more readily. Ideally, new fish should be quarantined before being introduced to an established aquarium, but failing this facility, a suitable preparation should be added to the water to guard against the development of *Oodinium* and similar diseases.

Acanthurus leucosternon.

Zebrasoma desjardini.

FAMILY ACANTHURIDAE: TANGS; SURGEONFISH

The common description of surgeonfish results from the presence of the two sharp spines, which are located either side of the caudal peduncle, near the base of the tail in many species. These spines when erected at right-angles to the body can be used to attack rivals. Since they can inflict serious injuries on each other, tangs are usually kept individually in aquaria, yet will often live agreeably in the company of other similar-sized fish.

Zebrasoma flavescens.

Many tangs are strikingly colourful fish, which may grow quite large. The Powder Blue Surgeon (*Acanthurus leucosternon*) is a typical example, which can attain a size of 30 cm (12 in) and thus needs a relatively large aquarium if it is to be seen to best effect. In common with other members of the family, algae or a suitable substitute will form an important part of its diet. The *Zebrasoma* species often available include the Yellow Tang (*Z. flavescens*) and the Sailfin Tang (*Z. desjardini*), which can both be aggressive by nature. Tangs of the genus *Naso* differ from the previous species by possessing pairs of rigid spines in the region of the caudal peduncle. Some also have an unusual pointed growth above the mouth, resembling the horn of the mythical unicorn, when adult. This characteristic is seen in the Short-nosed Unicorn Tang (*N. brevirostris*) which is otherwise a relatively dull fish, being greyish overall in colour.

FAMILY APOGONIDAE: CARDINALFISH

Members of this family are often red in colour. The Pyjama Cardinal (*Apogon orbicularis*) is often available, and can be kept in small groups quite successfully. It only reaches about 10 cm (4 in) in size. Cardinalfish are not active by nature, and often remain stationary, moving only when the light intensity falls. Some species are known to be mouth brooders, like certain freshwater cichlids, the male caring for the eggs in this way.

FAMILY BALISTIDAE: TRIGGERFISH

Triggerfish have relatively large heads, yet surprisingly small mouths, which contain powerful, sharp teeth. These are used to feed largely on invertebrates in the wild, and so shrimps and other shellfish should be included in their diet. Triggerfish often prove aggressive amongst themselves, and with other fish, and so are best housed individually. A number of species are imported, with the striking Clown Trigger (*Balistoides niger*) always commanding a high price when available. It is perhaps the most colourful member of the group, although others, such as the hardy Picasso Trigger (*Rhineacanthus aculeatus*) also have attractive markings. They can become quite tame, and may feed from the hand. The species *Odonus niger* occurs in several colour forms, and is named accordingly, depending on whether it is predominantly blue, green or black. Not surprisingly, the triggerfish have a wide range, being found in the Indo-Pacific region as well as the Red Sea. Those from the latter environment need to be kept in water with a higher SG, about 1.025. The Bursa Trigger (*Sufflamen bursa*) is worth considering as an introduction to the family, being one of the cheaper members and less aggressive than related Triggers.

FAMILY BLENNIIDAE: BLENNIES

Blennies have a wide distribution, with species being found in both temperate and tropical seas. The colourful Cardinal Blenny (*Blennius nigriceps*) occurs in Mediterranean waters, attaining a size of 4 cm ($1\frac{1}{2}$ in). These fish generally are easy to cater for, and can be kept in a community tank without problems.

Rhinecanthus aculeatus.

Balistoides niger.

They do not attract the attention given to some families but will spawn quite frequently, the male being responsible for guarding the eggs. At this time, other males will be kept away from the area, around the rocks where the eggs are normally laid.

FAMILY CANTHIGASTERIDAE: PUFFERFISH

The fish in this family are popularly known as pufferfish, since they will inflate their bodies when threatened, and even emit a croaking sound. They feed largely on invertebrates with tough shells, and their modified jaws can crush the hard exoskeleton of living corals. Amongst the species often available is the Valentine Puffer (*Canthigaster valentini*), which does best in relatively warm water, at a temperature of about 29°C (84°F). Young individuals are more colourful than adults, having a pattern of orange and blue dots on their flanks. Spots of various colours also occur in other species, which are generally smaller, averaging about 10 cm (4 in) in size.

FAMILY CHAETODONTIDAE: BUTTERFLYFISH AND ANGELFISH

This large family is sub-divided into the Butterflyfish, belonging to the sub-family Chaetodinae, and the Angelfish comprising the sub-family Pomacanthinae. Many species are popular inhabitants of marine aquaria, but butterflyfish are not always easy to establish successfully. They feed largely on invertebrates and will damage similar creatures kept alongside them in a tank. It is vital when purchasing butterflyfish to ensure that they are eating. If a fish refuses to eat, live brine shrimps may help to rekindle its appetite. Butterflyfish will also readily succumb to *Oodinium* infections, and since they can be rather sensitive to copper, an alternative remedy suitable for use with invertebrates should be obtained when they are introduced to a tank.

The Neon-banded Butterfly (*Chaetodon quadrimaculatus*) is one attractive species, often available from Pacific regions, which grows to a size of about 15 cm (6 in). Another good introduction to the group can be

Odonus niger.

provided by the popular Pakistan Butterfly (*C. collaris*), which has characteristic brown-purplish markings over its body and a broad white stripe both in front of and behind the eyes. The Addis Butterfly (*C. semilarvatus*) is a beautiful species from the region of the Red Sea, but is less readily available.

Some butterflyfish have elongated mouths, such as the Copperband species (*Chelmon rostratus*). Medium-sized fish are to be preferred, since young specimens need virtually constant feeding, while bigger individuals can be reluctant to eat, even when offered live brine shrimps or coral. These long-nosed fish delight in probing 'living rock' in search of tasty morsels, once they are established.

Angelfish, not to be confused with the freshwater fish of the same name, are one of the most colourful groups of marine fish, but unfortunately prove aggressive with each other, and so should be kept separately. Young fish often have a different pattern of markings compared to those of adults, and this may help to prevent them being attacked by their elders. Out of the larger species, the Blue Angelfish (*Pomacanthus annularis*) is a relatively easy species to establish, apart from being quite attractive. The Queen Angelfish (*Holacanthus ciliaris*) is an impressive fish, which can reach a size of 45 cm (18 in) and does well on a diet which includes some vegetable matter. The most striking and expensive of these large Angelfish is the Imperial or Emperor (*P. imperator*), which occurs in Indo-Pacific waters. It is quite susceptible to *Benedenia*. These fish seek shelter in caves and similar surroundings when frightened, and cover of this type should be accessible to them in the aquarium. The difference in coloration between adult and juvenile forms, (which is a characteristic of this genus), meant that, for a period, the latter were thought to be a different species.

The smaller 'Dwarf' Angelfish are no less attractive than their bigger relatives. The Flame Angelfish (*Centropyge loriculus*) is a vivid orange-red, with darker markings, and comes from the area around Hawaii. It can usually be kept safely in a community tank, but is always an expensive acquisition. The related Pygmy or Cherub Angelfish (*C. argi*) reaches a size of about 6 cm ($2\frac{1}{4}$ in), with the form known as *C. fisheri* growing slightly larger. The predominantly yellow Lemonpeel Angelfish (*C. flavissimus*) can also be recommended for the community tank, growing to about 10 cm (4 in) in length. Another highly desirable species is the Fire-ball or Flame-back (*C. acanthops*), being a combination of black and orange-red, which can generally be kept safely with invertebrates, but, like related species, is likely to destroy any *Caulerpa* in its aquarium.

Chaetodon quadrimaculatus.

Chaetodon collaris.

Chaetodon semilarvatus.

Pomacanthus annularis, with a moray-eel (below).

Above, *Holacanthus ciliaris*

Below, *Centropyge loriculus.*

FAMILY DIODONTIDAE: PORCUPINE PUFFERS

These fish are called Porcupine Puffers, because not only can they inflate themselves when threatened, but also their sharp spines become a further deterrent to potential predators. They tame easily, and their lively characters, coupled with their relative hardiness, make them appealing to the novice marine aquarist. Various species are available and some, notably tropical species such as *Diodon hystrix* can reach a size of 86 cm (35 in) in the wild, where they often occur in the company of Soldierfish (*see* Holocentridae). Porcupine Puffers will destroy invertebrates, which form part of their normal diet, and will take a variety of other foods in the aquarium.

FAMILY GOBIIDAE: GOBIES

Gobies are characterized by their modified pectoral fins, which act as suckers, holding them in place on suitable rockwork. Many species are not particularly active by nature, and do well in a relatively small aquarium. They have also been bred successfully under these conditions, the eggs often being laid in empty shells. The nest is guarded by the adult fish until the fry emerge about eleven days later. Unfortunately, the fry are likely to be eaten by their parents, unless they are moved to a separate rearing tank. Young gobies need a suitably fine food before being offered brine shrimps.

One of the cheapest and most colourful species is the Neon Goby (*Gobiosoma oceanops*), which is a combination of vivid blue and black stripes, occurring naturally in the Caribbean region. Slightly more expensive and less common now is the Catalina Goby (*Lythrypnus dalli*), which can prove rather territorial if kept with its own kind. It grows to about 4 cm ($1\frac{1}{2}$ in), and can fall victim to any larger crustaceans present in the tank.

FAMILY HOLOCENTRIDAE: SQUIRRELFISH; SOLDIERFISH

Squirrelfish are often predominantly red in colour and nocturnal by nature. They therefore need to be kept in relatively dark surroundings, with ample cover being provided by rockwork. Their alternative name of Soldierfish stems from the sharp spines present on the gill plates. They are carnivorous by nature, and should not be kept with smaller fish, which may be eaten, but can live together in groups. There are several species often available, ranking amongst the least costly of marine fish, with the Bigeye Squirrelfish (*Myripristis murdjan*) being one of the most attractive, in view of its vivid red coloration. The large eyes of this species assist its vision under conditions of low light intensity.

FAMILY LABRIDAE: WRASSES

This family is comprised of over 400 species, a number of which occur in tropical areas. They make undemanding aquarium occupants, accepting most types of food, but can grow very fast. Some species undergo a stunning colour change as they mature. The young Clown Wrasse (*Coris gaimardi*) is rather reminiscent of a Clownfish of the genus *Amphiprion*, being a combination of orange, black and white, but in older specimens, these markings disappear, and the body becomes duller, with vivid blue streaking appearing on the head. This species is sometimes confused with the African Clown Wrasse (*C. formosa*), which will bury itself under conditions of darkness in the floor of the aquarium.

In the case of the Birdnose or Birdmouth Wrasse (*Gomphosus coeruleus*), the sex of the individual fish will become apparent once they are adult, because of distinctive colour differences. Males turn bluish-

Coris gaimardi.

Monodactylus argenteus.

green, while females remain brown like juveniles. Vegetable matter forms a vital part of the diet of these active fish, which can attain 30 cm (12 in) in length. The Cleaner Wrasse (*Labroides dimidiatus*) is valued because it will take parasites off other fish in the tank, but it can harass some fish, and should not be kept alongside species such as the Boxfishes (Ostraciidae), which produce a poison when threatened.

FAMILY MONACANTHIDAE: FILEFISH

Filefish are similar to Triggerfish (Balistidae) in certain respects, but will live in a community tank if kept with other quiet fish, such as gobies or seahorses. The Orange-spotted Filefish (*Oxymonacanthus longirostris*) is sometimes imported from the Indo-Pacific region, but has rather specialized feeding habits. In the wild, it lives largely on coral polyps, and is not therefore an easy fish to maintain under aquarium conditions. It must be offered livefood almost exclusively, and live coral may have to be provided in the first instance, along with brine shrimps, to encourage a reluctant individual to start eating. These filefish are best kept in a small group. Its spine serves to anchor the fish in amongst corals, protecting it from predators. The rather duller Common Filefish (*Cantherhines sandwichiensis*) is generally easier to cater for, but may choose to nip the fins of companions in a mixed tank.

FAMILY MONODACTYLIDAE: MONOS

The Mono (*Monodactylus argenteus*) often lives in brackish waters when young, and makes an ideal introduction to marine fish-keeping. These fish will eat almost anything, ranging from dried food to brine shrimps, and will live in groups without fighting, growing to a size of about 22.5 cm (9 in). The related species, *M. sebae*, is found close to the shoreline of West Africa, and even in freshwater rivers.

FAMILY OSTRACIIDAE: BOXFISH; COWFISH

The popular names used for these fish reflect the shape of their box-like bodies. Boxfish belonging to the genus *Ostracion* are a potential hazard in an aquarium, however, because they can secrete a toxic mucus if threatened. In the confines of a tank, the concentration of the poison could endanger the lives of all the inhabitants. The Thornback Boxfish or Hovercraft (*Tetrasomus gibbosus*) is less likely to display this trait and proves both a hardy and an easily-tamed fish.

The Cowfish (*Lactoria cornuta*), so-called because of its apparent horns, has been spawned successfully in aquaria. Its pigmented eggs float on the water's surface and hatch within five days. Green algae and plankton make acceptable rearing foods, before the young can be weaned on to brine shrimps. They may reach a size of 50 cm (20 in), but rarely grow beyond 15 cm (6 in) under aquarium conditions. Cowfish need to be kept alongside gentle species if they are housed in a community tank. These fish will take a varied diet, including dried food.

Lactoria cornuta.

FAMILY PLATACIDAE: BATFISH

The elegance and personality of the Batfish have made it a popular aquarium inhabitant. Three species are usually available, with the Red-face Batfish (*Platax pinnatus*) commanding the highest price. It is also the most colourful form, especially when young, being a vivid black with contrasting red edging around its body. This Batfish has gained a reputation for being reluctant to feed initially, but once this hurdle has been overcome, it will prove a long-lived fish, and often becomes tame enough to feed from the hand. Their rate of growth is very rapid, and can be as much as 2.5 cm (1 in) per month, with adults reaching a maximum size of 45 cm (18 in).

The Orbiculate Batfish (*P. orbicularis*) is often easier to acclimatize to aquarium surroundings, although less colourful than the Red-face species. The Round-fin Batfish (*P. teira*) needs a relatively deep tank, in view of its highly elongated fins and rapid rate of growth. Members of the family Chaetodontidae are suitable companions for batfish, if they are not kept on their own. Squid torn into small pieces may encourage a reluctant batfish to start eating, and established fish will take almost any food of this type.

FAMILY PLECTORHYNCHIDAE: SWEETLIPS

Sweetlips will spend much of their time near the bottom of the aquarium, searching the substrate for food particles. Oriental Sweetlips (*Plectorhynchus orientalis*) often appear on dealers' lists. Younger fish of this species have more striking markings, being a combination of brown and pale yellow, with some deeper orange barring on their bodies. The Clown Sweetlips or Polkadot Grunt (*Gaterin chaetodonoides*) is sometimes available, and is essentially brown with white patches, which decrease in size as the fish gets older. They may grow to 30 cm (12 in) or so.

FAMILY POMACENTRIDAE: DAMSEL (DEVIL) FISH AND CLOWN (ANEMONE) FISH

These fish are commonly divided into two groups, the damsel or devilfish, and the clownfish. Damsels, better known as devils in the United States, are hardy, colourful and inexpensive. Unfortunately, they are also aggressive towards each other, especially in the case of older specimens. The attractive Neon Damsel (*Abudefduf oxyodon*) is a popular species which can grow to about 15 cm (6 in). The Electric Blue Damsel (*A. cyanae*) is colourful and typically undemanding with regard to its feeding requirements. Pairs in this instance can be distinguished because the male has a black edging to its caudal fin. Spawning in the aquarium is not unknown; the eggs are laid in suitable hiding places such as the insides of big shells. Once the fry hatch, they should be transferred to separate accommodation for rearing. This species is one of the more tolerant Damselfish in a community tank.

Many damsels become duller as they grow older. The young of the Orange-tail Damsel (*Paraglydion nigroris*) are a striking combination of rich blue with an orange tail, but turn brownish as they get older. Other, less colourful species include the Three-spot

Platax orbicularis, adult.

Abudefduf oxyodon.

Amphiprion sebae.

Humbug (*Dascyllus trimaculatus*), which are nevertheless hardy, and can encourage new additions in an aquarium to start feeding once the tank is established.

The Clownfish occur naturally in the company of various anemones, possessing a protective mucus which renders them immune to the stinging tentacles which are capable of killing other fish. They do well under aquarium conditions, but should be kept with a suitable anemone, particularly for spawning purposes. Various Clownfish have been bred successfully in aquaria, the fry being reared in a small separate tank with a ready supply of food constantly accessible to them. Brine shrimp nauplii can be introduced to their diet from the age of five days onwards.

The Chocolate or Yellow-tailed Anemone Fish (*Amphiprion clarkii*; formerly *A. sebae*) makes an ideal introduction to the group. It can grow up to 15 cm (6 in) in length, and is best kept either on its own, or as a group. Pairs will agree, but two fish of the same sex housed together often fight. Whenever possible, a *Stoichactes* or *Radianthus* anemone should be included in their aquarium, although these bigger Clownfish can be maintained without an anemone being present.

The Common Clown (*A. ocellaris*) is one of the species which is predominantly orange, with black and white striping on their bodies. They lay on clean rockwork close to the anemone, guarding the eggs until they hatch after a period of nine days. These clownfish can do well in a community tank, taking a wide variety of foodstuffs. The Pink Skunk Clown (*A. perideraion*) is considered the hardest species to maintain successfully, and must be kept with an anemone in its tank. Males in this case possess orange edging around their tail fins, and spawning has taken place under aquarium conditions. These fish reach a maximum size of about 7.5 cm (3 in).

Dascyllus trimaculatus.

FAMILY SCARIDAE: PARROTFISH

The description of 'parrotfish' was coined from the apparent beak and bright colours of these fish. They grow quite large, and can be difficult to maintain successfully in aquaria. Parrotfish graze naturally on living corals, and will not always accept a substitute readily. They can often be sexed easily by means of coloration differences, but are likely to prove aggressive in a community tank. These factors make them rather specialized fish in aquarium terms.

FAMILY SCATOPHAGIDAE: SCATS; MUCK-EATERS

The Spotted Scat (*Scatophagus argus*), with its yellowish body colour and black spots, is also known less flatteringly as the Hundred-eyed Muck-eater, because of its scavenging habits. Numbers are often found foraging for debris in waters close to human settlement throughout the Indo-Pacific region. It is a versatile fish, able to live in both brackish and saltwater, and can be kept without difficulty alongside other active fish in a community tank. A natural modification to the basic colour pattern is seen in the case of the Tiger Scat (*S. argus* var. *rubrifrons*), which has a reddish tinge to its body.

FAMILY SCORPAENIDAE: LIONFISH; SCORPIONFISH

The spectacular members of this family possess modified dorsal fin rays, which contain poison to catch unwary predators. A number of species are usually available. The Peacock Lionfish (*Pterois volitans*) is reputed to produce the most deadly venom. It adapts quite well to aquarium life, and soon takes inanimate food, whereas the Spot-fin Lionfish (*P. antennata*) may refuse to eat anything but livefood, such as young guppies. All *Pterois* species inhabit dark environments, and must be kept in low light. Excessively bright light may lead to blindness in these fish. The majority of species grow to about 25 cm (10 in) and although they can live alongside suitably large fish, it is possibly

Pterois lunulata.

safest to keep them on their own. Care must also be taken when servicing their aquarium not to be caught by the venomous fin rays.

Pterois radiata.

Pterois volitans.

FAMILY SERRANIDAE: GROUPERS; REEF COD

The Groupers or Reef Cod belong to this family, and can grow to a huge size in some cases. The majority cannot be kept in a community tank because they are highly predatory by nature. The Comet Grouper (*Calloplesiops altivelis*) is an exception, which will live satisfactorily with fish of a similar size. It may grow to 30 cm (12 in) and needs a suitably dark hiding place in the tank where it can retreat at first, although generally it becomes quite tame, and is easy to maintain on a varied diet, with a carnivorous bias.

FAMILY SYNGNATHIDAE: SEAHORSES AND PIPEFISH

The instantly-recognizable seahorses form part of this family, along with the pipefish. Over thirty separate species of seahorses are known, with some even occurring in English waters. They are normally sold simply as seahorses, rather than as distinct species. Reference to a specialized text is likely to be necessary for accurate identification. Seahorses are best kept on their own, since they are unable to compete with most other fish for food. They need unlimited supplies of livefoods, such as brine shrimps and small guppies as well as plankton. Their tank should include corals and similar decor, which the seahorses can anchor themselves to, via their tails.

Their breeding habits are especially fascinating. The eggs are passed from the female to the male, and then stored in the brood pouch. After about two months, the young emerge over the course of several days, and up to 600 have been reported from a single hatching. Most seahorses are relatively small, but the Oceanic species (*Hippocampus kuda*) from the Indo-Pacific region can be as large as 30 cm (12 in) in certain localized parts of its range.

Pipefish are available less often than seahorses. They have an equally unusual shape, being extremely long and thin. Males again possess a brood pouch, where the eggs are kept until they hatch. Pipefish feed by means of their long snouts, through which they suck up minute crustaceans, and require a similar diet to seahorses when kept in aquaria. The Zebra or Banded Pipefish (*Dunckerocampus dactyliophorus*) is one of the more colourful species, with perhaps twenty or so brownish-black rings, separated by horn-coloured bands running the length of its body.

FAMILY TETRAODONTIDAE: PUFFERFISH

Pufferfish belonging to the genus *Arothron* must not be kept with invertebrates, since they will destroy them, especially crustaceans, which form a significant part of their diet in the wild. They are relatively inactive fish, and will rest for periods on the floor of the aquarium. The Striped Puffer (*A. hispidus*), beloved by Japanese gourmets, in spite of much of its body being poisonous, will adapt well to aquarium surroundings. Amongst other species, the Black-spotted Puffer (*A. nigropunctatus*) is sometimes available, and has similar habits, readily using its sharp teeth on any living coral in the tank alongside it. These puffers all have prickly skins, and therefore should be handled cautiously if necessary. Other pufferfish are classified in the families Canthigasteridae and Diodontidae.

11 MARINE INVERTEBRATES

This diverse group of creatures are generally sensitive to the state of the water when kept in aquaria. While some will agree alongside each other, certain types must be kept apart or even isolated. Particular care also needs to be taken to ensure that they will live in harmony with fish in the aquarium, since many fish prey on invertebrates. In a mixed tank containing invertebrates, it is vital not to introduce water with a new fish. Many dealers medicate their aquaria as a precaution against *Oodinium* and similar infections,

Top left, White-banded cleaner prawn. **Top right**, Sea-urchin (*Tripneustes gratilla*). **Bottom left**, A bivalve mollusc (*Lima* sp.). **Bottom right**, Red hermit-crab (*Dardanus megistos*).

Variously coloured ceriantharians, with a starfish (*Protoreaster lincki*).

using copper-based remedies. The introduction of treated water containing this chemical will be disastrous for established invertebrates. The residual effects can last for as long as three months, and this should be borne in mind if, conversely, invertebrates are moved to a tank containing fish. There are, however, various safe remedies which can be used alongside invertebrates.

Many marine invertebrates are colourful and bizarre. The following section gives a brief indication of the major groupings, and species which are regularly seen. In many cases, these creatures will consume food given to fish, but complete diets are available for more fastidious invertebrates, such as the various filter-feeders.

COELENTERATES

This group of invertebrates encompasses the various types of coral and anemone, as well as the jellyfish. Sea anemones are probably the most popular members of the phylum and have a wide distribution throughout the oceans of the world. The tropical forms usually imported can make demanding tank occupants. They require well-oxygenated, moving water, yet should not be exposed to direct currents, which can cause them to shift their position in the tank. Sea anemones also require long periods of high intensity light, in order to maintain the micro-algae which live inside them and are essential for their well-being.

The anemones available for the marine aquarium can be divided into two categories. Those belonging to the Order Ceriantharia are often described as Sand or Tube Anemones because they keep their bodies buried or in the substrate, constructing a protective tube from whence they unfurl their long tentacles. If threatened, however, they rapidly withdraw. The venom produced by *Cerianthus* is quite potent, and will kill unwary small fish. These anemones are easily fed, by means of suitable products used for fish, put in the water above their tentacles. They need feeding only once or twice a week, and if overfed, produce unpleasant pellets which will pollute the tank.

The symbiotic group of anemones which support the *Amphiprion* Clownfish are harder to establish in the aquarium. Both *Discosoma* and *Stoichactis* are often available, in a variety of colours, from white through pink and green to blue and purple. Under good conditions, they can grow quite large, attaining a size of 45 cm (18 in) across. *Radianthus* species require a similar diet, and although Caribbean in origin, will readily provide shelter for Clownfish, which do not naturally occur in this region. Anemones may produce living young, which remain attached for a period to the adult by means of a slender thread. They are vulnerable to other creatures in the tank at this stage. For rearing purposes, brine shrimps or very finely chopped inert foodstuffs should be provided.

Many corals, like anemones, have living algae within their bodies, and thus require daily periods of prolonged lighting if they are to thrive in an aquarium. Although some species are filter-feeders, and must be treated accordingly, others will take slightly larger food. Regular water changes will be essential for corals, since, apart from being very sensitive to nitrite, the hard forms also remove lime from the water to build their protective casings. The pH of the water should be maintained at a figure of approximately 8.2. Other invertebrates, such as many crustaceans, as well as fish, will destroy living coral if given an opportunity.

Soft corals include the gorgonians, which feed during hours of daylight. The alcyonarians include the colourful Sea Whips and Fans. These are another group of soft corals which have an outer layer of soft tissue, where the polyps are located, and occur in a variety of colours. Good aeration is necessary for aquaria housing these and other corals.

Jellyfish are not ideal tank occupants, being highly specialized, with stinging tentacles in some cases, and prove rather fragile. *Cassiopeia* species are most often kept, living largely on the floor of the aquarium, rather than nearer the surface. Brine shrimp nauplii are again to be recommended for feeding these coelenterates.

A sea-anemone (*Radianthus*) with a symbiotic prawn (*Periclimenes*).

Cleaner prawn (*Stenopus hispidus*).

CRUSTACEANS

Crustaceans rank amongst the easiest of the marine invertebrates to maintain successfully in an aquarium, but larger species, such as the various coloured lobsters, are destructive and should be kept on their own, in spacious surroundings. A number of crabs are often available, and, like other members of this group, can prove useful scavengers, while possessing an unwelcome aggressive side to their natures. Hermit crabs, such as the Red form (*Dardanus megistos*), require a selection of suitable shells to be present in the tank, so that they can transfer to larger shells as they grow in size. Crustaceans moult at regular intervals, shedding their complete body casing. They require a pH of about 8.3, otherwise this process is likely to be impaired.

The predatory prawn (*Hymenocera picta*) eating a starfish (*Protoreaster lincki*).

Various colourful shrimps or prawns are the least troublesome of the crustaceans; indeed the Cleaner Prawn (*Stenopus hispidus*) actually removes debris from the sides of fish. They are largely nocturnal by nature, remaining concealed under rocks and similar hiding places during the daytime. Other species live protected by anemones, such as the aptly-named Anemone Shrimp (*Periclimenes* species). The small Harlequin Prawn (*Hymenocera picta*), in contrast, must not be kept with starfish, because it will destroy them.

ECHINODERMS

A variety of creatures of different shapes belong to the phylum Echinodermata. They include the starfish, sea-urchins and sea-cucumbers, examples of which can be kept in marine tanks. Starfish are not sedentary creatures, as their appearance may suggest, but move by means of tube feet, which have suckers at their ends to anchor the body in place, enabling them to climb vertically. They can be divided into two groups for aquarium purposes: those which have wide arms are more predatory than species with rounded arms, and are likely to attack bivalve molluscs and other invertebrates kept alongside them. Species belonging to the genus *Linckia* are perhaps the best choice – the Blue Starfish (*L. laevigata*) is often available.

Sea-urchins generally prove harder to maintain than starfish, needing both good quality water and a ready supply of algae. Signs of impending illness are shown by drooping spines, followed by subsequent loss and death. Sea-urchins are mobile, and possess longer feet than starfish. Those species with bigger spines are less often seen, because they are difficult to transport, and some produce poisons.

A feather-star which, like the sea-cucumbers, belongs among the echinoderms.

Feather-stars, also known as Crinoids, are fragile creatures, with arms resembling the tail feathers of a bird. These readily break off, which can handicap the unusual swimming action of these creatures. They are largely nocturnal and should be offered fine particles of food.

The Sea-cucumbers are more sedate, and can be quite variable in coloration, some forms possessing colourful tentacles, which serve to catch particles of

Orange and blue sponges with a red sea-urchin.

food present in the water. The tentacle with the food attached is then drawn into the body, and cleaned off. If threatened, sea-cucumbers may eject their internal organs, but this does them no apparent harm, and they recover eventually. They can be offered food intended for filter-feeding invertebrates.

A sea-cucumber or holothurian: two views to show the attractive crown of tentacles.

MOLLUSCS

Although a vast number of species are classified as belonging to the phylum Mollusca, there are four categories of particular interest to the marine aquarist. The univalve molluscs include the Tiger Cowrie (*Cypraea tigris*) and related species such as *C. mappa.* They have a single shell protecting their bodies. In

A tiger cowrie (*Cypraea tigris*) showing (below) the shell completely covered by the mantle, and (bottom) the shell partially exposed by the withdrawal of the mantle.

the aquarium, these cowries will forage happily, consuming algae and any food left by the fish. Some gastropods can be more aggressive, however, and members of the Cone family should be avoided because they are poisonous and capable of killing fish.

Bivalve molluscs available to the aquarist include clams and scallops. Special food is produced for these filter-feeders, and although not particularly colourful, they add character to a tank. The Flame Scallop (*Lima scabia*) is a particularly striking species when its bright red interior is revealed. They possess eyes which are sensitive to light, and are capable of moving to escape a potential predator, such as a starfish. Scallops can close their two shells tightly by means of a powerful adductor muscle, but a determined starfish can, in time, prise a division between them.

Nudibranch molluscs are often very attractive but prove difficult to keep as their feeding habits are usually specialized. They have no external shell, and some forms are free-swimming. Octopuses also belong to the phylum Mollusca, but are delicate creatures to maintain in the aquarium. They require a well-covered aquarium, in order to prevent them climbing out, and water which is of top quality, since even nitrate levels above 20 ppm can have fatal consequences. Some species are poisonous, and when faced with potential danger, they may produce their toxic 'ink', which turns the water cloudy. Octopuses should therefore be kept on their own, in relatively dark surroundings, with suitable hiding places readily accessible to them. Their food should consist largely of various crustaceans.

SEGMENTED SEA WORMS (ANNELIDA)

The Feather-duster Worms are named after the appearance of their feather-like gill filaments, and can occur in a range of colours. They live in tubes, extending tentacles to catch passing food particles, and then retreat back into their hiding places. These worms may be inadvertently introduced to the aquarium on 'living rock', but will soon be consumed by any fish present. The provision of brine shrimp nauplii, or a filter-feeder's diet, suits them well. They always seem to leave their tubes prior to death.

SPONGES (PORIFERA)

Sponges are variable in appearance, orange forms often being seen in aquaria. They are filter-feeders, and must be fed accordingly, on a suitable diet. Water conditions need to be good, and lighting should be minimal, since algal growth will block their pores, leading to death. Pieces broken off from an existing sponge will give rise to new colonies when transferred to another part of the aquarium. Sponges are farmed commercially along these lines, although they can also reproduce by sporulation.

An orange-red sponge.

SOME USEFUL ADDRESSES

British Cichlid Association,
33 Kirkmeadow,
Bretton,
Peterborough

British Killifish Association,
63 Huddersfield Road,
Newhey,
Rochdale,
Lancashire, OL16 3QZ

British Marine Aquarist Association,
16 Fountain Drive,
Roberttown,
Liversedge,
West Yorkshire, WF15 7PX

Catfish Association of Great Britain,
3 Spencer Avenue,
Hove,
East Sussex

When writing to any of the above organisations, a stamped, addressed envelope should be enclosed for a reply. The addresses given are correct at the time of going to press.

BIBLIOGRAPHY

The following titles may be useful for further reading:

Alder, H.E., *Fish Behaviour: Why Fishes do what they do*, (T.F.H.)
Axelrod, H.R. & Burgess, W.E., *Cichlid Fishes of Lakes Malawi and Tanganyika*, (T.F.H.)
Axelrod, H.R., *et al*, *All about Discus*, (T.F.H.)
Axelrod, H.R., *et al*, *Exotic Marine Fishes*, (T.F.H.)
Bellomy, M.D., *Encyclopedia of Seahorses*, (T.F.H.)
Emmens, C.W. & Axelrod, H.R., *Catfish*, (T.F.H.)
Emmens, C.W., *Guppy Handbook*, (T.F.H.)
Friese, U.E., *Marine Invertebrates*, (T.F.H.)
Goldstein, R.J., *Anabantoids: Gouramis and Related Fish*, (T.F.H.)
Goldstein, R.J., *Cichlids of the World*, (T.F.H.)
Gordon, M. & Axelrod, H.R., *Swordtails for the Advanced Aquarist*, (T.F.H.)
Hargreaves, V.B., *The Tropical Marine Aquarium*, (David & Charles)
Haywood, M., *Popular Marine Fish for Your Aquarium*, (Foulsham)
Hervey, G.J. & Hems, J., *The Goldfish*, (Faber & Faber)
Masters, C.O., *Encyclopedia of Live Foods*, (T.F.H.)
Mayland, H.J. & Vevers, G., *The Complete Home Aquarium*, (Ward Lock)
Myers, G.S., *The Piranha Book*, (T.F.H.)
Orme, F.W., *Fancy Goldfish Culture*, (Saiga Publishing)
Rataz, K. & Horeman, T., *Aquarium Plants*, (T.F.H.)
Schroder, J., *Genetics for the Aquarist*, (T.F.H.)
Sterba, G., *The Aquarist's Encyclopaedia*, (Blandford Press)
Stodola, J., *Encyclopedia of Water Plants*, (T.F.H.)

Periodicals of interest:
The Aquarist and Pondkeeper
Practical Fishkeeping
Tropical Fish Hobbyist

(Any of the above can be ordered from branches of W. H. Smith)

GENERAL INDEX

Page numbers in *italics* refer to illustrations.

INDEX OF FISH SPECIES

Page numbers in *italics* refer to illustrations.